הִנֵּנִי

THE NEW
HEBREW THROUGH PRAYER

3

Terry Kaye

Contributing Authors:
Claudia Grossman
Lori Justice

BEHRMAN HOUSE, INC.

The publisher gratefully acknowledges the cooperation
of the following sources of photographs for this book:

Ginny Twersky cover, 21; Gila Gevirtz 5, 16, 31, 37, 64, 72, 82, 87, 91; Creative Image 6, 41, 47, 51, 66, 84;
Sheila Plotkin 11; Richard Lobell 15, 79; Israel Ministry of Tourism 34;
Terry Kaye 55, 69; Hallmarc Photo 61

Torah Mantle, 25: Peachy Levy, Santa Monica, 1991; wool, embroidered and appliqued with
cotton and metallic thread; Museum commission—HUCSM

Book and Cover Composition: Pronto Design Inc.
Artist: Ilene Winn-Lederer

TABLE OF CONTENTS

אֵין כָּמוֹךְ אַב הָרַחֲמִים

אֵין כָּמוֹךְ

How do you feel when your friend gives you the latest CD you've been wanting for your birthday? You're probably excited and say a big "thanks!" The Jewish people regard the Torah as a precious gift, one for which we say thank you to God each time we read it. We express this gratitude in two prayers said just before the Ark is opened and the Torah is removed for the Torah service.

The first of these two prayers, אֵין כָּמוֹךְ, proclaims God's uniqueness. In it, we praise God for the power and the kindness that are God's alone—as well as for the strength and peace with which God blesses us. This prayer also communicates our belief that only God could have given us the precious gift of the Torah. Later in this chapter, we will learn about the second prayer said before the Ark is opened—אַב הָרַחֲמִים.

Practice reading אֵין כָּמוֹךְ aloud.

1. אֵין כָּמוֹךְ בָאֱלֹהִים, יְיָ, וְאֵין כְּמַעֲשֶׂיךָ. מַלְכוּתְךָ מַלְכוּת
2. כָּל עוֹלָמִים וּמֶמְשַׁלְתְּךָ בְּכָל דוֹר וָדֹר.
3. יְיָ מֶלֶךְ, יְיָ מָלָךְ, יְיָ יִמְלֹךְ לְעוֹלָם וָעֶד. יְיָ עֹז לְעַמוֹ יִתֵּן,
4. יְיָ יְבָרֵךְ אֶת־עַמוֹ בַשָׁלוֹם.

There is none like You, Adonai, among the gods (other people worship), and there are no deeds like Yours. Your sovereignty is an eternal sovereignty, and Your reign is from generation to generation.

Adonai is Ruler, Adonai ruled, Adonai will rule forever and ever. May Adonai give strength to our people, may Adonai bless our people with peace.

אֵין

(there is) none

כָּמוֹךָ

like you

(כְּ)מַעֲשֶׂיךָ

(like) your deeds

מַלְכוּתֶךָ

your sovereignty

וּמֶמְשַׁלְתְּךָ

and your reign

מֶלֶךְ

(is) ruler

מָלָךְ

ruled

יִמְלֹךְ

will rule

ALL YOURS

Many words in the אֵין כָּמוֹךָ prayer end in the suffix ךָ.
Connect each word below to its English meaning.

(like) your deeds   כָּמוֹךָ

and your reign   (כְּ)מַעֲשֶׂיךָ

like you   מַלְכוּתֶךָ

your sovereignty   וּמֶמְשַׁלְתְּךָ

Can you describe the most precious gift you've ever received?

PAST, PRESENT, FUTURE

Each word next to יְיָ below is built on the root מלכ ("rule").
Next to each line, write whether it is the past, present, or future tense.

tense:

_____   יְיָ יִמְלֹךְ

_____   יְיָ מָלָךְ

_____   יְיָ מֶלֶךְ

5

TORAH SERVICE

What do you like about going to the movies with your friends? Maybe it's the popcorn. Or maybe it's getting seats together and talking until the lights go out. Or maybe you can't wait to see the coming attractions. But the part we all look forward to the most—the highlight of our experience—is seeing the movie itself! In the same way, the Torah service is the highlight of all the prayers in our synagogue service, many of which come from the Torah (for example, שְׁמַע, וְאָהַבְתָּ, and מִי כָמֹכָה).

The Torah is the first part of the Hebrew Bible. In it we read the stories of our ancestors. But the Torah is far more than a textbook like the one you study in history class. Not only does it tell the story of our ancestors, it also symbolizes our connection to them and to God. In the thousands of years since we received the Torah, the Jewish people have been reading it over and over again, passing down its teachings from generation to generation.

Most congregations read a portion of the Torah on Shabbat morning and on certain Jewish holidays. Others read from the Torah on Friday evenings. In some congregations, a portion of the Torah is read on Mondays and Thursdays, too. The Torah service itself has three main parts: taking the Torah out of the Ark, reading the Torah, and returning the Torah to the Ark. Each part of the Torah service has its own blessings and ceremonies.

Parents and children can work together to better understand the teachings of our tradition.

Prayer Building Blocks

אֵין כָּמוֹךָ בָאֱלֹהִים "there is none like you among the gods (other people worship)"

אֵין means "(there is) none."

כָּמוֹךָ is made up of two parts:

כְּמוֹ means "like."

ךָ is a suffix meaning "you" or "your."

Sometimes, when you add a suffix to a word, it changes the word's letters or vowels (כְּמוֹ + ךָ = כָּמוֹךָ).

בָאֱלֹהִים means "among the gods."

בָ is a prefix meaning "among the" or "in the."

אֱלֹהִים means "gods."

The word "gods" has a small "g" because it refers to pagan gods that people worshipped in ancient times. We write the name of our God with a capital "G" because there is only One God.

The Sh'ma expresses this belief:

שְׁמַע יִשְׂרָאֵל: יְיָ אֱלֹהֵינוּ, יְיָ אֶחָד.

Write the English meaning of the Sh'ma below.

_____

DID YOU NOTICE?

The Torah service begins with a reference to God, not to the Torah itself. Why do you think the Torah service praises God first?

_____

_____

וְאֵין כְּמַעֲשֶׂיךָ "and there are no deeds like yours"

אֵין, we know, means "(there is) none."

The prefix וְ means _____.

כְּמַעֲשֶׂיךָ means "like your deeds."
We have just learned that the word כְּמוֹ means "like."
כְּ, the shorter form of the word כְּמוֹ, also means "like."

מַעֲשֶׂיךָ means "your deeds."
מַעֲשֶׂיךָ is built on the root עשׂה.
(*Note: Sometimes a root letter doesn't appear in a Hebrew word.*)

עשׂה tells us that "do" or "make" is part of a word's meaning.

The suffix ךָ means "you" or "your."

Circle the root letters in each word below.

שֶׁעָשָׂה   יַעֲשֶׂה   עֹשֶׂה   לְמַעֲשֶׂה

Now circle the words built on the root עשׂה in the prayer below.

עֹשֶׂה שָׁלוֹם בִּמְרוֹמָיו, הוּא יַעֲשֶׂה שָׁלוֹם עָלֵינוּ,
וְעַל כָּל-יִשְׂרָאֵל. וְאִמְרוּ אָמֵן.

How many words did you circle? _____

Do you recognize the prayer? Write its name here. _____

What does עֹשֶׂה שָׁלוֹם mean? _____

8

יְיָ מֶלֶךְ, יְיָ מָלָךְ, יְיָ יִמְלֹךְ לְעוֹלָם וָעֶד

**"Adonai is ruler, Adonai ruled,
Adonai will rule forever and ever"**

The word מֶלֶךְ means "ruler" or "is ruler."

Read these words:

יִמְלֹךְ   מָלָךְ   מֶלֶךְ

Each word is built on the root מלכ ("rule").

Reread the prayer on page 4 and circle all the words built on the root מלכ.

How many words did you circle? _____

FROM THE SOURCES

The prayer phrase יְיָ מֶלֶךְ, יְיָ מָלָךְ, יְיָ יִמְלֹךְ לְעוֹלָם וָעֶד is a compilation of verses from different parts of the Bible.

Read each biblical verse below and circle the phrase that appears in אֵין כָּמוֹךָ. (*Remember: God's name can be written as יְיָ or יְהֹוָה.*)

Psalm 10:16	יְהֹוָה מֶלֶךְ עוֹלָם וָעֶד 16 אָבְדוּ גוֹיִם מֵאַרְצוֹ:

Psalm 96:10	אִמְרוּ בַגּוֹיִם ׀ יְהֹוָה מָלָךְ 10 אַף־תִּכּוֹן תֵּבֵל בַּל־תִּמּוֹט יָדִין עַמִּים בְּמֵישָׁרִים:

Exodus 15:18	יְהֹוָה ׀ יִמְלֹךְ לְעֹלָם וָעֶד: 18

There is no single verse in the Bible that says God is, was, and will always be Ruler, yet the prayer expresses all these ideas in one sentence. Why do you think the prayer combines all these thoughts?

_____

_____

אַב הָרַחֲמִים

Whom do you trust most? You count on your mom or dad for lots of things—like helping you with your homework, cheering for you at your music recital, taking care of you when you're sick. You rely on your swim coach to teach you how to dive safely. And you depend on your best friend for everything from standing by you when you have a tough problem to telling you that your new outfit looks awesome!

The Jewish people put their trust in God to always be there for them. אַב הָרַחֲמִים, the second prayer recited as the Ark is opened for the Torah service, praises God for God's complete trustworthiness and mercy, and asks God to protect Jerusalem.

Practice reading אַב הָרַחֲמִים **aloud.**

1. אַב הָרַחֲמִים, הֵיטִיבָה בִרְצוֹנְךָ אֶת־צִיּוֹן;
2. תִּבְנֶה חוֹמוֹת יְרוּשָׁלָיִם.
3. כִּי בְךָ לְבַד בָּטָחְנוּ, מֶלֶךְ אֵל רָם וְנִשָּׂא,
4. אֲדוֹן עוֹלָמִים.

Merciful Parent, favor Zion with Your goodness;
rebuild the walls of Jerusalem.
For in You alone do we trust, sovereign God, high and exalted,
eternal Ruler.

הָרַחֲמִים

merciful, the mercy

יְרוּשָׁלָיִם

Jerusalem

בָּטָחְנוּ

we trust(ed)

WHAT'S MISSING?

Complete each prayer phrase with the missing word.

אַב _____

<u>merciful</u> parent

תִּבְנֶה חוֹמוֹת _____

rebuild the walls of <u>Jerusalem</u>

כִּי בְךָ לְבַד _____

for in you alone do <u>we trust</u>

When you're wrestling playfully with your brother, he trusts you not to hurt him.

MERCIFUL PARENT

In this prayer, we call God אַב הָרַחֲמִים ("merciful parent"). The root of הָרַחֲמִים is רחם ("mercy" or "compassion").

God is sometimes referred to by three other names, all expressing the idea that God is compassionate. The names are:

אֵל מָלֵא רַחֲמִים   God full of mercy

הָרַחֲמָן   the merciful one

אֵל רַחוּם וְחַנּוּן   compassionate and gracious God

Circle the root letters רחם in each of God's names above.

FROM THE SOURCES

אַב הָרַחֲמִים asks God to favor Zion (Jerusalem) with goodness and to rebuild it.

These words are taken from Psalm 51, which was written 2,500 years ago, just after the destruction of the First Temple in 586 B.C.E.

Below is an excerpt from Psalm 51. Underline the words that appear in אַב הָרַחֲמִים.

> 19 זִבְחֵי אֱלֹהִים רוּחַ נִשְׁבָּרָה
>
> לֵב־נִשְׁבָּר וְנִדְכֶּה
>
> אֱלֹהִים לֹא תִבְזֶה:
>
> 20 הֵיטִיבָה בִרְצוֹנְךָ אֶת־צִיּוֹן
>
> תִּבְנֶה חוֹמוֹת יְרוּשָׁלָ͏ִם:

WHOM DO YOU TRUST?

The prayer ends with the statement that we put our trust in God:

כִּי בְךָ לְבַד בָּטָחְנוּ

Think of somebody you trust. On the lines below, describe an incident or the character traits that make that person trustworthy.

_____

_____

_____

_____

_____

_____

FLUENT READING

Below is the unofficial anthem of the State of Israel—הַתִּקְוָה. Based on a poem written in 1878 by Naftali Herz Imber, it expresses the hope that the Jewish people would someday return from exile to live in their homeland—אֶרֶץ יִשְׂרָאֵל.

Practice reading הַתִּקְוָה.

Circle צִיּוֹן and יְרוּשָׁלַיִם each time they appear. How many words did you circle?_____

כָּל עוֹד בַּלֵּבָב פְּנִימָה
נֶפֶשׁ יְהוּדִי הוֹמִיָּה
וּלְפַאֲתֵי מִזְרָח קָדִימָה
עַיִן לְצִיּוֹן צוֹפִיָּה.

עוֹד לֹא אָבְדָה תִּקְוָתֵנוּ
הַתִּקְוָה בַּת שְׁנוֹת אַלְפַּיִם
לִהְיוֹת עַם חָפְשִׁי בְּאַרְצֵנוּ
אֶרֶץ צִיּוֹן וִירוּשָׁלַיִם.

Within the heart
a Jewish spirit is still alive
and the eyes look eastward
toward Zion.

Our hope is not lost,
the hope of two thousand years
to be a free nation in our land,
in the land of Zion and Jerusalem.

כִּי מִצִּיּוֹן לְךָ יְיָ

כִּי מִצִּיּוֹן

Which objects, or things that you do, link you to your past *and* to your future? If your mom gives you her wedding dress to wear when you get married, and you pass that dress on to your own daughter, you have created a chain linking your past and your future together. If your dad gives you his vintage baseball cards, and you someday give them to your own son or daughter, you also create such a chain. In the same way, the Torah links us to our ancestors and to our descendants. From generation to generation, the teachings of the Torah are passed down as we read it each week, creating an unending chain of knowledge and tradition, and building our heritage.

כִּי מִצִּיּוֹן, the prayer that we say as we remove the Torah from the Ark, connects us to our ancient past and to our future. It expresses our hope and our belief that both the Torah and the land of Israel will continue to be our source of spiritual strength for generations to come.

We stand as the Ark is opened.
Practice reading כִּי מִצִּיּוֹן aloud.

1. כִּי מִצִּיּוֹן תֵּצֵא תוֹרָה, וּדְבַר־יְיָ מִירוּשָׁלָיְם.

2. בָּרוּךְ שֶׁנָּתַן תּוֹרָה לְעַמּוֹ יִשְׂרָאֵל בִּקְדֻשָּׁתוֹ.

For out of Zion shall go forth Torah, and the word of God from Jerusalem.
Praised is the One, who in holiness gave the Torah to God's people Israel.

PRAYER DICTIONARY

מִצִּיּוֹן
from Zion

תּוֹרָה
Torah, teaching

וּדְבַר
and the word of

מִירוּשָׁלָיִם
from Jerusalem

שֶׁנָּתַן
who gave

לְעַמּוֹ
to God's people

בִּקְדֻשָּׁתוֹ
in God's holiness

MATCH GAME

Connect each Hebrew word to its English meaning.

to God's people   תּוֹרָה

from Zion   וּדְבַר

and the word of   מִירוּשָׁלָיִם

from Jerusalem   מִצִּיּוֹן

in God's holiness   שֶׁנָּתַן

who gave   לְעַמּוֹ

Torah, teaching   בִּקְדֻשָּׁתוֹ

With each tender act, parents can instill in their children an ability to love and nurture.

PRAYER VARIATIONS

As the Ark is opened, some congregations add the following words from the Torah (Numbers 10:35) before כִּי מִצִּיּוֹן.

וַיְהִי בִּנְסֹעַ הָאָרֹן וַיֹּאמֶר מֹשֶׁה:
קוּמָה יְיָ וְיָפֻצוּ אֹיְבֶיךָ, וְיָנֻסוּ מְשַׂנְאֶיךָ מִפָּנֶיךָ.

When the Ark was carried forward, Moses said:
Arise, Adonai; may Your enemies be scattered, may Your foes be driven to flight.

Other congregations do not mention war or the Jews' enemies, but add:

הָבוּ גֹדֶל לֵאלֹהֵינוּ וּתְנוּ כָבוֹד לַתּוֹרָה.

Let us declare God's greatness and give honor to the Torah.

No matter which words they add before כִּי מִצִּיּוֹן, all congregations are alike in praising God for giving us the Torah. Which version of the prayer is found in *your* synagogue's prayer book?

15

WHAT'S MISSING?

Circle the word that completes each sentence.

1. כִּי _____ תֵּצֵא תוֹרָה
   from Zion

   מִצִּיּוֹן   מִירוּשָׁלַיִם   לְעַמּוֹ

2. וּדְבַר יְיָ _____
   from Jerusalem

   תוֹרָה   מִירוּשָׁלַיִם   מִצִּיּוֹן

3. בָּרוּךְ שֶׁנָּתַן _____
   Torah

   יְיָ   יִשְׂרָאֵל   תוֹרָה

4. לְעַמּוֹ בִּקְדֻשָּׁתוֹ _____
   Israel

   יִשְׂרָאֵל   מִצִּיּוֹן   וּדְבַר

OUT OF ORDER

Number the seven words from the first line of כִּי מִצִּיּוֹן in the correct order.

תוֹרָה ◯   וּדְבַר ◯   תֵּצֵא ◯

מִירוּשָׁלַיִם ◯   מִצִּיּוֹן ◯

כִּי ◯   יְיָ ◯

Number the six words from the second line of כִּי מִצִּיּוֹן in the correct order.

לְעַמּוֹ ◯   יִשְׂרָאֵל ◯

בָּרוּךְ ◯   שֶׁנָּתַן ◯

בִּקְדֻשָּׁתוֹ ◯   תוֹרָה ◯

King David's Tower in the Old City of Jerusalem.

16

TORAH READING

How did the custom of reading the Torah originate?

Some of the Jews who had been in exile in Babylonia after the destruction of the First Temple in 586 B.C.E. were allowed to return to the land of Israel. But years had passed, and they and their children had forgotten the teachings of the Torah.

Around 400 B.C.E, Ezra the scribe, determined to rebuild Jewish life in Israel, stood during Rosh Hashanah in front of the gathered Jews and read to them from the Torah. The Jews cried when they heard the words of the Torah again.

They returned the next day to study Torah, and they celebrated Sukkot for the first time in many years. But Ezra knew they would have to be reminded of the meaning of the Torah if they were to live according to its laws. So he arranged public Torah readings on Mondays and Thursdays, on Shabbat, and on certain holidays.

Why on Mondays and Thursdays? Those were market days, when the people came together in large numbers to do business.

And to this day—thousands of years later—many congregations still read from the Torah in the synagogue on Mondays and Thursdays, and on certain holidays, in addition to Shabbat.

Answer the questions below:

• How did reading aloud from the Torah in public help the Jews in Ezra's time?

_____

_____

• Why do you think it is important to continue this tradition?

_____

_____

Prayer Building Blocks

מִצִּיּוֹן "from Zion"

מִצִּיּוֹן is made up of two parts.

מִ is a prefix meaning "from."

צִיּוֹן means "Zion."

מִצִּיּוֹן means _____.

Zion is another name for Jerusalem.

וּדְבַר "and the word of"

וּ is a prefix meaning _____.

דְּבַר means "the word of."

Read the following sentences and circle all the words built on the root דבר ("speak," "word," or "thing").

1. וְהָיוּ הַדְּבָרִים הָאֵלֶּה, אֲשֶׁר אָנֹכִי מְצַוְּךָ הַיּוֹם, עַל לְבָבֶךָ.

2. בָּרוּךְ אַתָּה יְיָ, הָאֵל הַנֶּאֱמָן בְּכָל דְּבָרָיו.

3. וְעֵינֵינוּ תִרְאֶינָה מַלְכוּתֶךָ כַּדָּבָר הָאָמוּר בְּשִׁירֵי עֻזֶּךָ.

4. וְדָבָר אֶחָד מִדְּבָרֶיךָ אָחוֹר לֹא יָשׁוּב רֵיקָם.

5. הָאֵל הַנֶּאֱמָן, הָאוֹמֵר וְעוֹשֶׂה, הַמְדַבֵּר וּמְקַיֵּם.

DID YOU KNOW?

In Hebrew, we refer to the Ten Commandments as עֲשֶׂרֶת הַדִּבְּרוֹת.

Circle the root letters דבר in the second word: עֲשֶׂרֶת הַדִּבְּרוֹת

What does עֲשֶׂרֶת mean? _____

מִירוּשָׁלַיִם "from Jerusalem"

מִירוּשָׁלַיִם is made up of two parts.

מִ is a prefix meaning "from."

יְרוּשָׁלַיִם means "Jerusalem."

The prophet Isaiah first said the words כִּי מִצִּיּוֹן תֵּצֵא תוֹרָה, וּדְבַר-יְיָ מִירוּשָׁלַיִם
in his vision of a peaceful world in which "they shall beat their swords into plowshares" and
"nation shall not lift up sword against nation" (Isaiah 2:3-4). Here, תוֹרָה means "teaching"
or "instruction."

Read these sentences and underline the Hebrew word for Jerusalem in each one.

1. וּבְנֵה יְרוּשָׁלַיִם עִיר הַקֹּדֶשׁ בִּמְהֵרָה בְיָמֵינוּ.

2. אַב הָרַחֲמִים, הֵיטִיבָה בִרְצוֹנְךָ אֶת צִיּוֹן,
   תִּבְנֶה חוֹמוֹת יְרוּשָׁלָיִם.

3. תִּתְגַּדַּל וְתִתְקַדַּשׁ בְּתוֹךְ יְרוּשָׁלַיִם עִירְךָ.

4. בָּרוּךְ אַתָּה יְיָ, בּוֹנֵה בְרַחֲמָיו יְרוּשָׁלָיִם, אָמֵן.

5. שִׂמְחוּ אֶת יְרוּשָׁלַיִם וְגִילוּ בָה כָּל אֹהֲבֶיהָ.

Do you recognize the prayer in line 2?

Write its name here. _____

When do we say this prayer? _____

שֶׁנָּתַן "who gave"

שֶׁנָּתַן is made up of two parts.

שֶׁ is a prefix meaning "who."

נָתַן means "gave."

בָּרוּךְ שֶׁנָּתַן תּוֹרָה means "praised is the One who gave the Torah."

Who is the One who gave us the Torah? Write your answer in Hebrew. _____

לְעַמּוֹ "to God's people"

לְ is a prefix meaning "to."

עַמּוֹ means "God's people."

עַם means "people" or "nation."

וֹ at the end of a word means "his."

As God is neither male nor female, we translate לְעַמּוֹ as "to God's people."

בִּקְדֻשָּׁתוֹ "in God's holiness"

בְּ is a prefix meaning "in."

קְדֻשָׁה means "holiness."

קְדֻשָׁתוֹ means "God's holiness."

בִּקְדֻשָּׁתוֹ means _____.

What is the root of בִּקְדֻשָּׁתוֹ? ____ ____ ____

Circle the root letters קדש in each word below.

קַדְּשֵׁנוּ   מַקְדִּישִׁים   הַקָּדוֹשׁ   וַיְקַדֵּשׁ

וּקְדוֹשִׁים   קָדוֹשׁ

What does קדש mean? _____

HOLDING THE TORAH

In many congregations, the person holding the Torah, after it is taken out of the Ark, recites each of the following lines, first alone, and then with the congregation. In other congregations, the lines are recited in unison.

שְׁמַע יִשְׂרָאֵל: יְיָ אֱלֹהֵינוּ, יְיָ אֶחָד.

Hear O Israel: Adonai is our God, Adonai is One.

אֶחָד אֱלֹהֵינוּ, גָּדוֹל אֲדוֹנֵינוּ, קָדוֹשׁ שְׁמוֹ.

Our God is One and is great; God's name is holy.

A third line is added. In some congregations, the person holding the Torah turns to face the Ark and bows when this line is recited.

גַּדְּלוּ לַיְיָ אִתִּי וּנְרוֹמְמָה שְׁמוֹ יַחְדָּו.

Acclaim Adonai with me, and together let us exalt God's name.

When you become a Bar or Bat Mitzvah you will have the honor of holding the most sacred possession of the Jewish people.

Have you ever stood and watched something exciting go by? Maybe you've been to a wedding where you can't take your eyes off the beautiful bride walking down the aisle. Or maybe you've gone to a basketball game where the players run into the arena through a tunnel and emerge to cheers as the crowd jumps to its feet. Or maybe you've arrived early at the Fourth of July parade so you can get a good spot to watch the bands and floats.

Traditionally, during the Torah service, we stand to watch the Torah as it is carried through the congregation, perhaps by the rabbi, or the cantor, a bar or bat mitzvah, or an honored congregant. As the Torah is carried up and down the aisles, from the Ark to the reader's table on the *bimah*, there is a feeling of anticipation. Everyone turns to keep the Torah in sight as a sign of respect to God. As the Torah passes by, we sing לְךָ יְיָ, a prayer that praises God's greatness.

Practice reading לְךָ יְיָ aloud.

1. לְךָ, יְיָ, הַגְּדֻלָּה וְהַגְּבוּרָה וְהַתִּפְאֶרֶת וְהַנֵּצַח וְהַהוֹד,

2. כִּי כֹל בַּשָּׁמַיִם וּבָאָרֶץ, לְךָ יְיָ הַמַּמְלָכָה וְהַמִּתְנַשֵּׂא לְכֹל לְרֹאשׁ.

Yours, God, is the greatness, the power, the glory, the victory, and the majesty; for all that is in heaven and earth is Yours. Yours is the sovereignty, God; You are supreme over all.

Read the English translation of the prayer above. Notice that we do not mention the Torah in the prayer. You might expect us to praise the Torah as we carry it lovingly from the Ark, but instead we praise God.

Why do we praise God instead of the Torah? Because, although we honor the Torah and respect it, we worship only God.

Why do you think this prayer encourages us to worship God and not the Torah?

_____

_____

FLUENT READING

Each line below contains a word you know. Practice reading the lines.

1. בָּרוּךְ אַתָּה, יְיָ, הָאֵל הַנֶּאֱמָן בְּכָל דְּבָרָיו.

2. אוֹר חָדָשׁ עַל צִיּוֹן תָּאִיר וְנִזְכֶּה כֻלָּנוּ מְהֵרָה לְאוֹרוֹ.

3. וּבְדִבְרֵי קָדְשְׁךָ כָּתוּב לֵאמֹר: יִמְלֹךְ יְיָ לְעוֹלָם אֱלֹהַיִךְ צִיּוֹן לְדֹר וָדֹר הַלְלוּיָהּ.

4. אִם אֶשְׁכָּחֵךְ יְרוּשָׁלָיִם תִּשְׁכַּח יְמִינִי.

5. גָּדוֹל יְיָ וּמְהֻלָּל מְאֹד וְלִגְדֻלָּתוֹ אֵין חֵקֶר.

6. כִּי בָנוּ בָחַרְתָּ וְאוֹתָנוּ קִדַּשְׁתָּ.

7. רְצֵה יְיָ אֱלֹהֵינוּ בְּעַמְּךָ יִשְׂרָאֵל וּבִתְפִלָּתָם.

8. הָאֵל הַגָּדוֹל הַגִּבּוֹר וְהַנּוֹרָא, אֵל עֶלְיוֹן.

9. בָּרוּךְ אַתָּה, יְיָ, הַבּוֹחֵר בַּתּוֹרָה, וּבְמֹשֶׁה עַבְדּוֹ, וּבְיִשְׂרָאֵל עַמּוֹ, וּבִנְבִיאֵי הָאֱמֶת וָצֶדֶק.

10. לִהְיוֹת עַם חָפְשִׁי בְּאַרְצֵנוּ, אֶרֶץ צִיּוֹן וִירוּשָׁלָיִם.

בִּרְכוֹת הַתּוֹרָה

Have you seen the Torah's elaborate cover and ornaments—its rich silver embroidery on fine fabric, tiny bells adorning brass or silver handle ornaments, and fancy breastplate? When the Torah reaches the reader's table after it has been carried through the congregation, the rabbi or Torah reader removes the covering and ornaments, sets the Torah on the table, and unrolls it to that week's פָּרָשָׁה—Torah portion.

Each *parashah* is divided into sections, or readings. For each section, one or more congregants are called up to the Torah to say two blessings—one before the Torah reader begins to read that section, and one after the reader has finished. The honor of being called up to recite these blessings is called an עֲלִיָּה ("going up"). The blessing before the Torah reading has two parts. The first part is the Bar'chu, a call to the congregation to praise God. The second part thanks God for choosing us to receive the gift of the Torah.

BLESSING BEFORE THE TORAH READING

Practice reading the blessing aloud.

1. בָּרְכוּ אֶת־יְיָ הַמְבֹרָךְ.

2. בָּרוּךְ יְיָ הַמְבֹרָךְ לְעוֹלָם וָעֶד.

3. בָּרוּךְ אַתָּה, יְיָ אֱלֹהֵינוּ, מֶלֶךְ הָעוֹלָם,

4. אֲשֶׁר בָּחַר־בָּנוּ מִכָּל־הָעַמִּים,

5. וְנָתַן־לָנוּ אֶת־תּוֹרָתוֹ.

6. בָּרוּךְ אַתָּה, יְיָ, נוֹתֵן הַתּוֹרָה.

Praise Adonai, who is praised.
Praised is Adonai, who is praised forever and ever.
Praised are You, Adonai our God, Ruler of the world,
for choosing us from all the nations
and giving us God's Torah.
Praised are You, Adonai, who gives us the Torah.

בָּחַר

chose (choosing)

בָּנוּ

us

מִכָּל

from all

הָעַמִּים

the nations

וְנָתַן

and gave (and giving)

לָנוּ

to us

תּוֹרָתוֹ

God's Torah

נוֹתֵן

gives

MATCH GAME

Connect each Hebrew word to its English meaning.

us	בָּחַר
and gave (and giving)	בָּנוּ
chose (choosing)	מִכָּל הָעַמִּים
to us	וְנָתַן
God's Torah	נוֹתֵן
gives	לָנוּ
from all the nations	תּוֹרָתוֹ

This Torah mantle is adorned with a quote from Leviticus 25:10, which also appears on the Liberty Bell in Philadelphia.

LETTER LINK

It is no easy task to read from the Torah. You must be trained to read Hebrew fluently, and without vowels or punctuation, in order to read without mistakes. What's more, in many synagogues the Torah portion is chanted using special musical inflections or melodies called trope. The Torah reader (בַּעַל קְרִיאָה, for a man or a boy; בַּעֲלַת קְרִיאָה, for a woman or a girl) often prepares for the reading by practicing in a *tikkun*, a book in which the words of the Torah appear twice—in one column they appear in regular Hebrew print with vowels and punctuation, and in the second column, the text looks just like the Torah itself.

Sometimes, the Torah reader is the Bar Mitzvah or Bat Mitzvah, whose family members are given the honor of an *aliyah*—reciting the blessings before and after the sections in the Torah reading. If you read Torah when you celebrate becoming Bar or Bat Mitzvah, *you* may learn how to read trope.

Here is the way Hebrew letters look in a Torah scroll.

אבגדהוזחטיכרלמסנןסעפּףצץקרשת

Connect each Torah letter below to the matching printed letter.

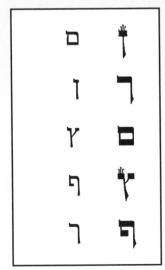  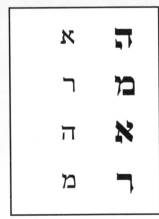 

Prayer Building Blocks

Read the first two lines of the Torah blessing. Do you recognize them?

1. בָּרְכוּ אֶת־יְיָ הַמְבֹרָךְ.

2. בָּרוּךְ יְיָ הַמְבֹרָךְ לְעוֹלָם וָעֶד.

The Torah reading begins with the בָּרְכוּ—the Call to Worship, the official opening of the prayer service. Why do you think the blessing before the Torah reading begins with the בָּרְכוּ?

_____

_____

Words built on the root ברכ have "praise" or "bless" as part of their meaning. Circle all the words in the בָּרְכוּ that are built on the root ברכ.

This root means _____ or _____.

Now read the next part of the Torah blessing.

1. בָּרוּךְ אַתָּה, יְיָ אֱלֹהֵינוּ, מֶלֶךְ הָעוֹלָם,

2. אֲשֶׁר בָּחַר־בָּנוּ מִכָּל־הָעַמִּים, וְנָתַן־לָנוּ אֶת־תּוֹרָתוֹ.

Underline the six words that are found at the beginning of most בְּרָכוֹת.

אֲשֶׁר בָּחַר בָּנוּ **"who chose us" ("for choosing us")**

אֲשֶׁר means "who."

בָּחַר means "chose."

בָּנוּ means "us."

Who chose us to receive the Torah? _____

To whom does "us" refer? _____

27

וְנָתַן לָנוּ אֶת תּוֹרָתוֹ

"and gave us God's Torah" ("and giving us God's Torah")

וְנָתַן means "and gave."

וְ is a prefix meaning _____.

נָתַן means _____ .

לָנוּ means "to us."

תּוֹרָתוֹ is made up of two word-parts: תּוֹרָה and the word ending וֹ ("his").

Because God is neither male nor female, we translate תּוֹרָתוֹ as "God's Torah."

What did God give us? _____

Write your answer in Hebrew. _____

CROSSWORD

Read the Hebrew clues and fill in the correct English words.

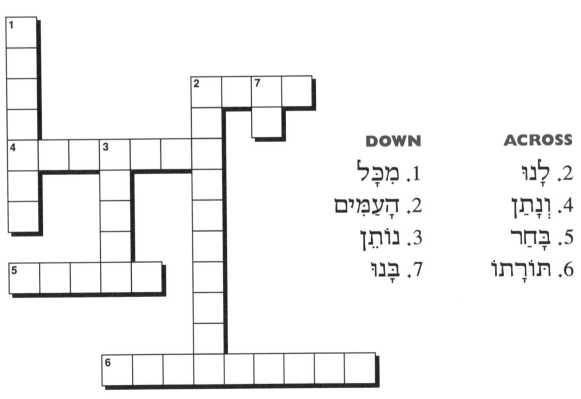

DOWN

‎1. מִכָּל

‎2. הָעַמִּים

‎3. נוֹתֵן

‎7. בָּנוּ

ACROSS

‎2. לָנוּ

‎4. וְנָתַן

‎5. בָּחַר

‎6. תּוֹרָתוֹ

FACTS AND FIGURES ABOUT THE TORAH READING

- The Torah (also called the Five Books of Moses) is divided into 54 portions (פָּרָשׁוֹת).

- It takes exactly one year to read the whole Torah. We begin reading the first book, Genesis (בְּרֵאשִׁית), on Simḥat Torah, and complete reading the last book, Deuteronomy (דְּבָרִים), one year later on the following Simḥat Torah. We then begin all over again.

- The last person called to the Torah on Shabbat is known as the *maftir* (for a man or a boy) or the *maftirah* (for a woman or a girl). This is often the Bar Mitzvah or Bat Mitzvah. The *maftir* or *maftirah* recites the blessings before and after the reading of the last few verses of the Torah portion, and then chants a portion from Prophets called the *haftarah*.

Answer the following questions:

1. How many portions (פָּרָשׁוֹת) are contained in the Torah? _____

2. On which holiday do we finish reading the Torah and begin all over again?

   _____

3. Explain what the *maftir* or *maftirah* does.

   _____

   _____

4. How do you think it feels to be the *maftir* or *maftirah*? Why?

   _____

   _____

BLESSING AFTER THE TORAH READING

The blessing we say after the Torah reader has finished reading that section of the Torah praises God for giving us the Torah of truth and eternal life. Although our bodies cannot live forever, by reading the Torah and passing it and its lessons down to our children and then to their children, we keep Torah and we keep our heritage alive forever. The chain of tradition that began when Moses and the Israelites received the Torah almost 3,500 years ago lives on as we hear its words each week.

Practice reading the blessing said after the Torah reading.

1. בָּרוּךְ אַתָּה, יְיָ אֱלֹהֵינוּ, מֶלֶךְ הָעוֹלָם,

2. אֲשֶׁר נָתַן־לָנוּ תּוֹרַת אֱמֶת

3. וְחַיֵּי עוֹלָם נָטַע בְּתוֹכֵנוּ.

4. בָּרוּךְ אַתָּה, יְיָ, נוֹתֵן הַתּוֹרָה.

Praised are You, Adonai our God, Ruler of the world,
who gave us the Torah of truth,
and implanted within us eternal life.
Praised are You, Adonai, who gives us the Torah.

30

תּוֹרַת

Torah of

אֱמֶת

truth

וְחַיֵּי

and life (of)

עוֹלָם

eternal, world

PHRASE MATCH

Connect each Hebrew phrase to its English meaning.

and eternal life	לְעוֹלָם וָעֶד
ruler of the world	תּוֹרַת אֱמֶת
forever and ever	וְחַיֵּי עוֹלָם
Torah of truth	מֶלֶךְ הָעוֹלָם

When we help someone in need, or perform any other mitzvah, we are keeping the words of the Torah alive.

WHAT'S MISSING?

Fill in the missing Hebrew words in the prayer.

בָּרוּךְ אַתָּה, יְיָ אֱלֹהֵינוּ, מֶלֶךְ הָעוֹלָם,

אֲשֶׁר נָתַן־לָנוּ _____ _____
                       Torah of truth

נָטַע בְּתוֹכֵנוּ _____ _____.
                   and eternal life

בָּרוּךְ אַתָּה, יְיָ, _____ הַתּוֹרָה.
                 gives

Prayer Building Blocks

אֲשֶׁר נָתַן לָנוּ תּוֹרַת אֱמֶת

"who gave us the Torah of truth"

נָתַן לָנוּ means _____.

תּוֹרַת אֱמֶת means "Torah of truth."

תּוֹרַת is a combination word that means "Torah of."

אֱמֶת means "truth."

Complete the Hebrew phrase: _____ אֲשֶׁר נָתַן לָנוּ

What did God give us? _____

Why do you think we refer to the Torah as "Torah of truth"?

_____

_____

וְחַיֵּי עוֹלָם **"and eternal life"**

וְחַיֵּי means "and a life of."

וְ is a prefix meaning _____.

חַיֵּי means "a life of."

The word for "life" is חַיִּים. (Do you know the toast "לְחַיִּים!"—"To Life!"?)

עוֹלָם means "eternal."

עוֹלָם also means "world."

וְחַיֵּי עוֹלָם means _____.

32

Read the following sentences and underline עוֹלָם in each one.

1. וְשִׁבְחֲךָ אֱלֹהֵינוּ מִפִּינוּ לֹא יָמוּשׁ לְעוֹלָם וָעֶד.

2. אֲדוֹן עוֹלָם אֲשֶׁר מָלַךְ בְּטֶרֶם כָּל יְצִיר נִבְרָא.

3. יִתְבָּרַךְ שִׁמְךָ בְּפִי כָל חַי תָּמִיד לְעוֹלָם וָעֶד.

4. וַאֲנַחְנוּ נְבָרֵךְ יָה מֵעַתָּה וְעַד עוֹלָם.

5. נְקַדֵּשׁ אֶת שִׁמְךָ בָּעוֹלָם, כְּשֵׁם שֶׁמַּקְדִּישִׁים אוֹתוֹ
בִּשְׁמֵי מָרוֹם.

6. אֵל חַי וְקַיָּם תָּמִיד יִמְלֹךְ עָלֵינוּ לְעוֹלָם וָעֶד.

CHALLENGE QUESTION

Reread the blessing on page 30.

Describe the theme—or main idea—of this blessing, which is recited after the Torah reading.

_____

_____

_____

ALIYAH

Why do we use the term עֲלִיָּה ("going up")? We *go up* to the *bimah* when we are called to recite the blessings before and after each section of the Torah reading. We also *go up* in the eyes of the congregation when we receive this honor. And we *go up*, or move closer, to God.

You may have heard the word עֲלִיָּה in a different context. Going to live in Israel is called עֲלִיָּה (we "make *aliyah*"). We don't just *move* to the Holy Land, we *go up* to it.

The number of עֲלִיּוֹת in each Torah portion depends on the day it is read. For example, on Mondays and Thursdays there are three עֲלִיּוֹת, on Yom Kippur there are six, and on Shabbat morning there are usually seven. The number of עֲלִיּוֹת indicates the level of holiness of the day. In this case, Shabbat is even holier than Yom Kippur!

In some congregations, each person honored with an *aliyah* receives a special blessing of well-being, called a מִי שֶׁבֵּרַךְ. In this blessing, we ask God to protect the person from illness and distress, and to bless him or her with good health and success. Another version of the prayer, said during the Torah service, asks for the well-being of sick congregants, their loved ones, and friends.

New immigrants making *aliyah* to the State of Israel

FLUENT READING

Each line below contains a word you know. Practice reading the lines.

1. בָּרוּךְ שֶׁנָּתַן תּוֹרָה לְעַמּוֹ יִשְׂרָאֵל בִּקְדֻשָּׁתוֹ.

2. יְהִי שֵׁם יְיָ מְבֹרָךְ, מֵעַתָּה וְעַד עוֹלָם.

3. הוּא נוֹתֵן לֶחֶם לְכָל בָּשָׂר.

4. תּוֹרָה וּמִצְוֹת, חֻקִּים וּמִשְׁפָּטִים אוֹתָנוּ לִמַּדְתָּ.

5. שֶׁכָּל דְּבָרָיו אֱמֶת וָצֶדֶק.

6. וְתִתֶּן לָנוּ חַיִּים אֲרֻכִּים, חַיִּים שֶׁל שָׁלוֹם,
חַיִּים שֶׁל טוֹבָה, חַיִּים שֶׁל בְּרָכָה.

7. כַּכָּתוּב בְּתוֹרָתֶךְ: יְיָ יִמְלֹךְ לְעֹלָם וָעֶד.

8. אֵין לָנוּ מֶלֶךְ אֶלָּא אָתָּה.

9. חַיִּים שֶׁתְּהֵי בָנוּ אַהֲבַת תּוֹרָה וְיִרְאַת שָׁמַיִם.

10. כִּי אַתָּה שׁוֹמֵעַ תְּפִלַּת עַמְּךָ יִשְׂרָאֵל.

בִּרְכוֹת הַהַפְטָרָה

The Torah is the first part of the Bible (תַּנַ"ךְ); the Book of Prophets (נְבִיאִים) is the second; and Writings (כְּתוּבִים), which includes psalms, poems, and proverbs, is the third. At the conclusion of the Torah reading on Shabbat and on holidays, an honored person in the congregation reads a section from the Book of Prophets called the הַפְטָרָה ("conclusion"). The haftarah is often related by theme to that week's Torah portion or to a holiday season. When you become a Bar or Bat Mitzvah and are called up to the Torah for the first time, you will be the one to chant the haftarah that day!

Our tradition teaches that the prophets were learned, righteous people who spread the word of the Torah to the Jewish people. They were the conscience of the Jews. The truths taught by the prophets are told in the haftarah and help us to better understand important ideas or values found in the Torah.

We say a blessing before chanting the haftarah. Because the prophets were so important in communicating God's word, this blessing praises God for the fact that the Israelites had prophets.

BLESSING BEFORE THE HAFTARAH READING

Practice reading the blessing aloud.

1. בָּרוּךְ אַתָּה, יְיָ אֱלֹהֵינוּ, מֶלֶךְ הָעוֹלָם, אֲשֶׁר בָּחַר

2. בִּנְבִיאִים טוֹבִים, וְרָצָה בְדִבְרֵיהֶם הַנֶּאֱמָרִים בֶּאֱמֶת.

3. בָּרוּךְ אַתָּה יְיָ, הַבּוֹחֵר בַּתּוֹרָה, וּבְמֹשֶׁה עַבְדּוֹ,

4. וּבְיִשְׂרָאֵל עַמּוֹ, וּבִנְבִיאֵי הָאֱמֶת וָצֶדֶק.

Praised are You, Adonai our God, Ruler of the world, who chose
good (faithful) prophets, and was pleased with their words spoken in truth.
Praised are You, Adonai, the One who takes delight in (chooses) the Torah, and in Moses, God's
servant, and in Israel, God's people, and in prophets of truth and righteousness (justice).

בָּחַר

chose

(בִּ)נְבִיאִים

prophets

טוֹבִים

good (faithful)

הַנֶּאֱמָרִים

spoken

בֶּאֱמֶת

in truth

הַבּוֹחֵר

the one who chooses

עַבְדּוֹ

God's servant

עַמּוֹ

God's people

וָצֶדֶק

and righteousness (justice)

THE FAMILY CONNECTION

There are three sets of related words in the blessing before the הַפְטָרָה reading.

3	2	1
בֶּאֱמֶת	בִּנְבִיאִים	בָּחַר
הָאֱמֶת	וּבִנְבִיאֵי	הַבּוֹחֵר

Write the number of the related words next to their English meaning.

_____ prophets

_____ choose

_____ truth

It may seem as though you find the number 13 everywhere you look in the year you become a Bar or Bat Mitzvah.

MAKE ME A MATCH!

Connect the Hebrew word to its English meaning.

God's people   טוֹבִים

and righteousness (justice)   הַנֶּאֱמָרִים

good (faithful)   עַבְדּוֹ

spoken   עַמּוֹ

God's servant   וָצֶדֶק

CLUE WORDS

The Hebrew name for the Bible— תַּנַ"ךְ —is an acronym. It is made up of the first letter in the name of each part of the Bible:

Torah   תּוֹרָה (תּ) .1

Prophets   נְבִיאִים (נ) .2

Writings   כְּתוּבִים (כ, ךְ) .3

Find the two Hebrew words that mean "prophets" in the blessing on page 36 and write them below.

_____   _____

DID YOU KNOW?

Both the Torah and the haftarah are chanted according to musical inflections (trope) shown by markings under and over the words themselves. But the tunes of the trope for the Torah and haftarah differ slightly.

While the Torah is chanted from a scroll that is rolled from one portion to the next, the haftarah is chanted from a printed book. On Simḥat Torah, when we finish reading the Torah for the year, it must be rerolled all the way from the end of the scroll back to the beginning in order to start over again!

PROPHET MATCH

Connect the Hebrew and English names of each prophet.

Micah   יִרְמְיָהוּ

Deborah   עָמוֹס

Zechariah   יְשַׁעְיָהוּ

Ezekiel   יְחֶזְקֵאל

Amos   דְּבוֹרָה

Jeremiah   מִיכָה

Isaiah   זְכַרְיָה

38

Prayer Building Blocks

אֲשֶׁר בָּחַר בִּנְבִיאִים טוֹבִים
"who chose good (faithful) prophets"

בָּחַר means "chose."

נְבִיאִים is the plural of נָבִיא.

Circle the part of נְבִיאִים that shows it is plural: נְבִיאִים

נָבִיא means _____.

נְבִיאִים means _____.

טוֹבִים is an adjective describing נְבִיאִים.

Circle the part of טוֹבִים that shows it is plural: טוֹבִים

טוֹב means _____.

טוֹבִים means _____.

הַנֶּאֱמָרִים בָּאֱמֶת "spoken in truth"

הַנֶּאֱמָרִים means "spoken."

The root letters of הַנֶּאֱמָרִים are אמר.

אמר means "speak" or "say."

בָּאֱמֶת means "in truth."

Read the following phrases aloud. Circle the words with the root אמר.

1. הָאֵל הַנֶּאֱמָן, הָאוֹמֵר וְעוֹשֶׂה

2. יִהְיוּ לְרָצוֹן אִמְרֵי פִי

3. חֲבֵרִים כָּל־יִשְׂרָאֵל, וְנֹאמַר אָמֵן

4. אָז יֹאמְרוּ בַגּוֹיִם: "הִגְדִּיל יְיָ לַעֲשׂוֹת עִם אֵלֶּה"

5. בָּרוּךְ שֶׁאָמַר וְהָיָה הָעוֹלָם, בָּרוּךְ הוּא

39

An Ethical Echo

Psalm 15 teaches us that telling the truth—אֱמֶת—is so important that only those who "speak truth in their hearts and have no slander on their tongues" will "live in God's house." The prophets, whose words we read in the haftarah, were also known as "prophets of truth," because they passed the truth of righteous and just behavior from God to the Jewish people.

Think About This!

It would be hard to find someone who's *never* told a lie! Maybe you ate a slice of the freshly baked apple pie meant for that night's dinner guests, and then pretended it wasn't you. Perhaps you forgot to walk the dog, but then claimed you did, so your dad wouldn't get upset. Or maybe you've joined in spreading false rumors about someone. What does the expression "to get caught in a web of lies" mean? In addition to being truthful to others, why do we need to be truthful to ourselves?

הַבּוֹחֵר בַּתּוֹרָה "the one who chooses the Torah"

הַבּוֹחֵר means "the one who chooses."

In this phrase, הַ is a prefix meaning "the one who."

בּוֹחֵר means _____.

הַבּוֹחֵר is built on the root בחר.

The root בחר tells us that "choose" is part of a word's meaning.

Below are lines from two prayers you have studied. Read each excerpt and circle all the words built on the root בחר. Then write the number of the line from each prayer next to the name of the prayer.

1. בָּרוּךְ אַתָּה, יְיָ אֱלֹהֵינוּ, מֶלֶךְ הָעוֹלָם, אֲשֶׁר בָּחַר־בָּנוּ מִכָּל־הָעַמִּים, וְנָתַן־לָנוּ אֶת־תּוֹרָתוֹ.

2. כִּי בָנוּ בָחַרְתָּ וְאוֹתָנוּ קִדַּשְׁתָּ מִכָּל הָעַמִּים

Kiddush _____

Blessing Before the Torah Reading _____

40

וּבְמֹשֶׁה עַבְדּוֹ "and Moses, God's servant"

וּבְמֹשֶׁה means "and Moses."

וּ is a prefix meaning _____.

מֹשֶׁה means _____.

עַבְדּוֹ means "God's servant."

עַבְדּוֹ is made up of two word-parts: עֶבֶד and the word ending וֹ ("his"). Because God is neither male nor female, we translate עַבְדּוֹ as "God's servant." In what ways was Moses God's servant?

_____

_____

When we are young, sometimes we are tempted to gossip or tell tales. As we mature, we begin to understand how hurtful such behavior can be.

וּבְיִשְׂרָאֵל עַמּוֹ "and Israel, God's people"

וּבְיִשְׂרָאֵל means "and Israel."

וּ means _____.

יִשְׂרָאֵל means _____.

עַמּוֹ means "God's people."

עַם means "people" or "nation."

וֹ at the end of a word means "his."

Because God is neither male nor female, we translate עַמּוֹ as "God's people."

וּבִנְבִיאֵי הָאֱמֶת וָצֶדֶק

"and prophets of truth and righteousness (justice)"

וּבִנְבִיאֵי means "and prophets of."

וּ means _____.

נְבִיאֵי means "prophets of."

הָאֱמֶת means "the truth."

הָ means _____.

אֱמֶת means _____.

Read the following prayer excerpts. Circle the word אֱמֶת in each line.

1. וְטַהֵר לִבֵּנוּ לְעָבְדְּךָ בֶּאֱמֶת

2. אֲשֶׁר נָתַן לָנוּ תּוֹרַת אֱמֶת וְחַיֵּי עוֹלָם נָטַע בְּתוֹכֵנוּ

3. אֱמֶת מַלְכֵּנוּ, אֶפֶס זוּלָתוֹ

4. תּוֹרַת אֱמֶת נָתַן לְעַמּוֹ אֵל עַל יַד נְבִיאוֹ נֶאֱמַן בֵּיתוֹ

5. הוֹלֵךְ תָּמִים וּפֹעֵל צֶדֶק וְדֹבֵר אֱמֶת בִּלְבָבוֹ

וָצֶדֶק means "and righteousness" or "and justice."

וָ means _____.

צֶדֶק means _____.

An Ethical Echo

The Hebrew word צְדָקָה comes from the word צֶדֶק ("righteousness" or "justice"). Giving tzedakah is a commandment and an obligation for all Jews. According to Jewish law, we should all give a portion of our earnings to those less fortunate. The highest level of tzedakah is when we give anonymously and so generously that a needy person can become self-sufficient.

Think About This!

What kinds of tzedakah—besides money—can we give? If you give food to a food bank or clothes to a clothing drive, is that tzedakah? Why? If you give a needy person a job, why is that considered the highest level of tzedakah? Do you think it is important to give tzedakah anonymously? Why or why not?

BLESSINGS AFTER THE HAFTARAH READING

When people you can count on—maybe your parent or your best friend—promise to do something, you usually rely on them because of your relationship and your trust. You believe your best friend's promise to keep it secret that you have a crush on that cute kid in math class. You believe your dad when he says he'll pick you up after the dance. Our tradition teaches us that the Jewish people have a relationship with God that is also built on trust, and that God watches over us, gives us life, and is merciful to us. We believe in God's promises.

We say four blessings after the haftarah reading. The first three blessings have to do with promises made by God to the Jewish people and our hope that those promises will come true.

The fourth and final blessing after the haftarah thanks God for the Torah, the worship service, the prophets, and Shabbat.

Practice reading the <u>first</u> of these blessings aloud.

1. בָּרוּךְ אַתָּה, יְיָ אֱלֹהֵינוּ, מֶלֶךְ הָעוֹלָם, צוּר כָּל הָעוֹלָמִים,

2. צַדִּיק בְּכָל הַדּוֹרוֹת, הָאֵל הַנֶּאֱמָן, הָאוֹמֵר וְעוֹשֶׂה,

3. הַמְדַבֵּר וּמְקַיֵּם, שֶׁכָּל־דְּבָרָיו אֱמֶת וָצֶדֶק.

4. נֶאֱמָן אַתָּה הוּא, יְיָ אֱלֹהֵינוּ, וְנֶאֱמָנִים דְּבָרֶיךָ, וְדָבָר אֶחָד

5. מִדְּבָרֶיךָ, אָחוֹר לֹא יָשׁוּב רֵיקָם, כִּי אֵל מֶלֶךְ נֶאֱמָן

6. וְרַחֲמָן אָתָּה.

7. בָּרוּךְ אַתָּה, יְיָ, הָאֵל הַנֶּאֱמָן בְּכָל־דְּבָרָיו.

Praised are You, Adonai our God, Ruler of the world, rock of all eternity,
righteous in all generations, the faithful God, the One who says and does,
the One who speaks and fulfills, for all God's words are truthful and just.

You are faithful, Adonai our God, and faithful are Your words, and not one of Your words
will return empty, for You are a faithful and compassionate God and Ruler.
Praised are You, Adonai, faithful in all Your words.

BLESSINGS GALORE!

You learned that the blessing before the haftarah praises God for choosing prophets who are faithful, who speak the truth, and who act justly.

The four blessings after the haftarah have very different themes. Read the theme for each blessing, then answer the question.

Blessing 1
praises God, whose words are true and who fulfills all promises.

Blessing 2
asks God to have mercy on and to protect Zion, and prays for our return there. In ancient times, Zion was another name for Jerusalem.

Blessing 3
asks God to reinstate the descendants of David as the rulers of the Jewish people.

Blessing 4
thanks God for: (1) the Torah, (2) the worship service, (3) the prophets, and (4) Shabbat, our holy day of rest.

How is the fourth blessing after the haftarah the high point of all the other blessings, including the blessing before the haftarah?

_____

_____

_____

DID YOU KNOW?

We are not sure exactly when the הַפְטָרָה blessings were composed. The *Amoraim*—the rabbis whose commentaries on Jewish law are recorded in the *Gemara*—first referred to these blessings around the year 300 C.E. So the haftarah blessings are at least 1,700 years old.

FLUENT READING

Practice reading blessings two, three, and four which are said after the הַפְטָרָה reading.

II

1. רַחֵם עַל־צִיּוֹן כִּי הִיא בֵּית חַיֵּינוּ, וְלַעֲלוּבַת נֶפֶשׁ תּוֹשִׁיעַ

2. בִּמְהֵרָה בְיָמֵינוּ. בָּרוּךְ אַתָּה, יְיָ, מְשַׂמֵּחַ צִיּוֹן בְּבָנֶיהָ.

III

3. שַׂמְּחֵנוּ, יְיָ אֱלֹהֵינוּ, בְּאֵלִיָּהוּ הַנָּבִיא עַבְדֶּךָ, וּבְמַלְכוּת בֵּית דָּוִד

4. מְשִׁיחֶךָ, בִּמְהֵרָה יָבֹא וְיָגֵל לִבֵּנוּ. עַל־כִּסְאוֹ לֹא־יֵשֶׁב זָר

5. וְלֹא־יִנְחֲלוּ עוֹד אֲחֵרִים אֶת־כְּבוֹדוֹ, כִּי בְשֵׁם קָדְשְׁךָ נִשְׁבַּעְתָּ

6. לוֹ שֶׁלֹּא־יִכְבֶּה נֵרוֹ לְעוֹלָם וָעֶד. בָּרוּךְ אַתָּה, יְיָ, מָגֵן דָּוִד.

IV

7. עַל־הַתּוֹרָה, וְעַל־הָעֲבוֹדָה, וְעַל הַנְּבִיאִים, וְעַל־יוֹם הַשַּׁבָּת הַזֶּה,

8. שֶׁנָּתַתָּ־לָּנוּ, יְיָ אֱלֹהֵינוּ, לִקְדֻשָּׁה וְלִמְנוּחָה, לְכָבוֹד וּלְתִפְאָרֶת,

9. עַל־הַכֹּל, יְיָ אֱלֹהֵינוּ, אֲנַחְנוּ מוֹדִים לָךְ, וּמְבָרְכִים אוֹתָךְ.

10. יִתְבָּרַךְ שִׁמְךָ בְּפִי כָּל־חַי תָּמִיד לְעוֹלָם וָעֶד.

11. בָּרוּךְ אַתָּה, יְיָ, מְקַדֵּשׁ הַשַּׁבָּת.

45

וְזֹאת הַתּוֹרָה עֵץ חַיִּים הִיא עַל שְׁלֹשָׁה דְבָרִים

וְזֹאת הַתּוֹרָה

What's the most recent honor you received that made you proud? Maybe it was a diploma, or a pennant from the county softball tournament, or a trophy for best project at the science fair. You might have held up your diploma for everyone to see, or taken a team photo with the pennant, or polished your trophy until it sparkled!

The Jewish people are proud of the Torah, and each time after it is read, we lift it up high so the congregation can see the inside of the scroll. The honor of lifting up the Torah is called *hagbahah*. We proudly raise the Torah to show symbolically that the words we just read aloud are the same words that Moses spoke to the Israelites in the wilderness almost 3,500 years ago.

Practice reading וְזֹאת הַתּוֹרָה aloud.

1. וְזֹאת הַתּוֹרָה אֲשֶׁר־שָׂם מֹשֶׁה לִפְנֵי בְּנֵי יִשְׂרָאֵל,
2. עַל־פִּי יְיָ בְּיַד־מֹשֶׁה.

*And this is the Torah that Moses placed before the people of Israel,
by the word of Adonai through Moses.*

Prayer Dictionary

וְזֹאת
and this is

שָׂם
placed, put

מֹשֶׁה
Moses

לִפְנֵי
before

בְּנֵי
people of

יִשְׂרָאֵל
Israel

SEARCH AND CIRCLE

Circle the Hebrew word that means the same as the English.

and this is	וְחַיֵּי עוֹלָם	וְזֹאת	וְנָתַן
placed, put	שָׁם	בָּחַר	עוֹשֶׂה
Moses	מֹשֶׁה	מֶלֶךְ	מִצִּיּוֹן
before	לָנוּ	לִפְנֵי	בָּנוּ
Israel	אֲבוֹתֵינוּ	לְעוֹלָם וָעֶד	יִשְׂרָאֵל

We hold the Torah up high for the entire congregation to see.

WHAT'S MISSING?

Fill in the missing Hebrew words to complete the prayer.

וְזֹאת ––––––– אֲשֶׁר־שָׂם ––––––––
לִפְנֵי בְּנֵי ––––––––, עַל־פִּי יְיָ
בְּיַד־ ––––––––.

Prayer Building Blocks

וְזֹאת הַתּוֹרָה "and this is the Torah"

וְזֹאת means "and this is."

וְ means _____.

זֹאת means _____.

הַ means _____.

וְזֹאת הַתּוֹרָה means _____.

FROM THE SOURCES

וְזֹאת הַתּוֹרָה is taken from the Torah. Below are three verses from the Torah. Find and underline all the words of וְזֹאת הַתּוֹרָה. (*Remember:* יְיָ *can also be written* יְהֹוָה.) Practice reading all the lines aloud.

Deuteronomy 4:44-45

44 וְזֹאת הַתּוֹרָה אֲשֶׁר־שָׂם
45 מֹשֶׁה לִפְנֵי בְּנֵי יִשְׂרָאֵל: אֵלֶּה הָעֵדֹת
וְהַחֻקִּים וְהַמִּשְׁפָּטִים אֲשֶׁר דִּבֶּר מֹשֶׁה
אֶל־בְּנֵי יִשְׂרָאֵל בְּצֵאתָם מִמִּצְרָיִם:

Numbers 9:23

23 אֶת־מִשְׁמֶרֶת יְהוָה שָׁמָרוּ עַל־פִּי יְהוָה בְּיַד־
מֹשֶׁה:

48

אֲשֶׁר־שָׂם מֹשֶׁה "that Moses placed"

שָׂם means "placed" or "put."

מֹשֶׁה means "Moses."

What did Moses place? Write your answer in Hebrew. _____

Read these sentences aloud and underline the Hebrew word for Moses in each one.

1. וַיְהִי בִּנְסֹעַ הָאָרֹן וַיֹּאמֶר מֹשֶׁה

2. לֹא קָם בְּיִשְׂרָאֵל כְּמֹשֶׁה עוֹד נָבִיא, וּמַבִּיט אֶת תְּמוּנָתוֹ

3. בָּרוּךְ אַתָּה יְיָ, הַבּוֹחֵר בַּתּוֹרָה וּבְמֹשֶׁה עַבְדּוֹ...
   וּבִנְבִיאֵי הָאֱמֶת וָצֶדֶק

4. תּוֹרָה צִוָּה לָנוּ מֹשֶׁה, מוֹרָשָׁה קְהִלַּת יַעֲקֹב

לִפְנֵי בְּנֵי יִשְׂרָאֵל "before the people of Israel"

לִפְנֵי means "before."

בְּנֵי יִשְׂרָאֵל means "the people of Israel."

Read the underlined part of this prayer:

וְזֹאת הַתּוֹרָה אֲשֶׁר־שָׂם מֹשֶׁה לִפְנֵי בְּנֵי יִשְׂרָאֵל,

עַל־פִּי יְיָ בְּיַד־מֹשֶׁה.

We translate these words as "by the word of Adonai through Moses."

- Circle the Hebrew word for Adonai in the underlined part of the Hebrew prayer above.

- Put a star above the Hebrew word for Moses.

- Whose words or mitzvot are contained in the Torah?
  Write your answer in Hebrew. _____

- Who brought those words or mitzvot to the people?
  Write your answer in Hebrew. _____

עֵץ חַיִּים הִיא

Before returning the Torah to the Ark, we roll it and dress it again in its cover and ornaments. The honor of rolling and dressing the Torah is called *g'lilah*.

As it is returned to the Ark, we sing עֵץ חַיִּים הִיא, a prayer of rich language and imagery comparing the Torah to a tree of life.

As a tree is a living thing, with roots that reach down into the earth and branches that reach up to the sun, so is the Torah a living thing symbolically. Its roots reach back to our ancestors who first received it and followed its commandments. Its branches are the generations that continue to read it and believe in its teachings. By carrying on the tradition of reading and studying Torah, and by passing that tradition on to future generations, we strengthen our roots and allow our Jewish heritage to grow, to flourish, and to live on forever.

Practice reading עֵץ חַיִּים הִיא **aloud.**

1. עֵץ־חַיִּים הִיא לַמַּחֲזִיקִים בָּהּ, וְתֹמְכֶיהָ מְאֻשָּׁר.

2. דְּרָכֶיהָ דַרְכֵי־נֹעַם, וְכָל־נְתִיבוֹתֶיהָ שָׁלוֹם.

It (the Torah) is a tree of life to those who uphold it, and those who support it are happy. Its ways are ways of pleasantness and all its paths are peace.

עֵץ

tree

חַיִּים

(of) life

מְאֻשָּׁר

happy

דְּרָכֶיהָ

its ways

דַּרְכֵי

ways of

נֹעַם

pleasantness

שָׁלוֹם

peace

MATCH GAME

Connect each Hebrew word to its English meaning.

pleasantness   עֵץ

its ways   מְאֻשָּׁר

ways of   דְּרָכֶיהָ

happy   דַּרְכֵי

tree   נֹעַם

This rabbi and cantor roll the Torah before dressing it and returning it to the Ark.

DESCRIPTIVE WORDS

Fill in the English meanings for the Hebrew words describing the Torah.

חַיִּים   _____

מְאֻשָּׁר   _____

נֹעַם   _____

שָׁלוֹם   _____

51

Prayer Building Blocks

עֵץ חַיִּים הִיא לַמַּחֲזִיקִים בָּה

"it is a tree of life to those who uphold it"

עֵץ means _____.

חַיִּים means _____.

Why do *you* think the Torah is compared to a tree?

_____

Fill in the missing words in English.

The Torah is a _____ to those who uphold it.

Now fill in the missing words in Hebrew.

_____ הִיא לַמַּחֲזִיקִים בָּה.

DID YOU KNOW?

The two wooden rollers to which the Torah parchment is attached are also called עֲצֵי חַיִּים (the plural of עֵץ חַיִּים), trees of life.

Why is this an appropriate name for the rollers?

_____

מְאֻשָּׁר "happy"

מְאֻשָּׁר means "happy."

אֹשֶׁר means "happiness."

Read the following lines aloud and circle the words meaning "happy."

אַשְׁרֵי יוֹשְׁבֵי בֵיתֶךָ עוֹד יְהַלְלוּךָ סֶּלָה.

אַשְׁרֵי הָעָם שֶׁכָּכָה לּוֹ אַשְׁרֵי הָעָם שֶׁיְיָ אֱלֹהָיו.

How many words did you circle? _____

52

דְּרָכֶיהָ דַרְכֵי נֹעַם "its ways are ways of pleasantness"

דְּרָכֶיהָ means "its ways."

דַרְכֵי means "ways of."

Both words are variations of דֶּרֶךְ ("road" or "way"). Circle the three letters meaning "road" or "way" in the words below.

דְּרָכֶיהָ   דַרְכֵי

Read the two sentences below and circle the words meaning "road" or "way."

1. צַדִּיק יְיָ בְּכָל דְּרָכָיו, וְחָסִיד בְּכָל מַעֲשָׂיו

2. בְּשִׁבְתְּךָ בְּבֵיתֶךָ וּבְלֶכְתְּךָ בַדֶּרֶךְ וּבְשָׁכְבְּךָ וּבְקוּמֶךָ

FROM THE SOURCES

עֵץ חַיִּים הִיא is taken from the תַּנַ"ךְ (Proverbs 3).

Below is the excerpt from Proverbs in which עֵץ חַיִּים הִיא is found.

Underline all the words of the עֵץ חַיִּים הִיא prayer. Then read the Biblical excerpt.

16 אֹרֶךְ יָמִים בִּימִינָהּ
בִּשְׂמֹאולָהּ עֹשֶׁר וְכָבוֹד:
17 דְּרָכֶיהָ דַרְכֵי-נֹעַם
וְכָל-נְתִיבוֹתֶיהָ שָׁלוֹם:
18 עֵץ-חַיִּים הִיא לַמַּחֲזִיקִים בָּהּ
וְתֹמְכֶיהָ מְאֻשָּׁר:

How does the order of the verses in the תַּנַ"ךְ differ from our version in the siddur?

53

עַל שְׁלשָׁה דְבָרִים

If someone were to ask you what three things you need in order to live, you might answer, "food, clothing, and shelter," or maybe "air, light, and water," or even "television, CDs, and computers"! But when we think in terms of our Jewish heritage, the answer is in the prayer עַל שְׁלשָׁה דְבָרִים.

This prayer tells us that as Jews, the three most important things our world depends on are Torah, worship, and acts of kindness. While food, clothing, shelter, and air keep our bodies alive, our souls, our heritage, and our strength as a people depend on these three things: the teachings of the Torah, believing in and serving God, and acts of goodness toward others.

Practice reading עַל שְׁלשָׁה דְבָרִים **aloud.**

1. עַל שְׁלשָׁה דְבָרִים הָעוֹלָם עוֹמֵד:

2. עַל הַתּוֹרָה וְעַל הָעֲבוֹדָה וְעַל גְּמִילוּת חֲסָדִים.

The world stands on three things:
On Torah, on worship, and on acts of loving-kindness.

עַל

on

שְׁלֹשָׁה

three

דְּבָרִים

things

הָעוֹלָם

the world

עוֹמֵד

stands

הַתּוֹרָה

the Torah

הָעֲבוֹדָה

the worship

גְּמִילוּת חֲסָדִים

acts of loving-kindness

FILL IN THE BLANKS

According to עַל שְׁלֹשָׁה דְּבָרִים, the world of Judaism stands on three pillars.

Write the English meaning above each Hebrew word below.

_____

הָעוֹלָם

_____   _____   _____

גְּמִילוּת חֲסָדִים   הָעֲבוֹדָה   הַתּוֹרָה

The very same computer you use to write an English paper or order a CD can become a "mitzvah machine" when you use it to search the web for organizations that help those in need.

WHAT'S WRONG?

Cross out the English words in each line that do *not* mean the same as the Hebrew. Think carefully!

the Ḥumash	the Five Books of Moses	the Torah	הַתּוֹרָה
the worship	the Torah	the praying	הָעֲבוֹדָה
our ancestors	good deeds	acts of loving-kindness	גְּמִילוּת חֲסָדִים

Prayer Building Blocks

עַל שְׁלֹשָׁה דְבָרִים **"on three things"**

עַל means _____.

שְׁלֹשָׁה means _____.

Fill in the missing Hebrew word below. Then read the numbers 1–10 in Hebrew.

10. עֲשָׂרָה	7. שִׁבְעָה	4. אַרְבָּעָה	1. אֶחָד
	8. שְׁמוֹנָה	5. חֲמִשָּׁה	2. שְׁנַיִם
	9. תִּשְׁעָה	6. שִׁשָּׁה	3. _____

דְבָרִים is the plural of דָבָר.

דָבָר means "thing."

דְבָרִים means "things."

Circle the part of the word that shows it is plural. דְבָרִים

הָעוֹלָם עוֹמֵד **"the world stands"**

הָעוֹלָם means "the world."

הָ means _____.

עוֹלָם means _____.

עוֹמֵד ("stands") is built on the root עמד.

The root of עֲמִידָה is ____ ____ ____.

How did the עֲמִידָה prayer get its name?

56

עַל הַתּוֹרָה "on the Torah"

We know that הַתּוֹרָה means "the Torah."

But הַתּוֹרָה is not just the scroll we read.

הַתּוֹרָה means studying the writings of the Torah and learning from it how to worship God (הָעֲבוֹדָה) and how to be a good person (גְּמִילוּת חֲסָדִים).

How can studying the Torah teach us how to act toward God and toward other people?

_____

_____

Read the בְּרָכָה that we say before studying the Torah.

בָּרוּךְ אַתָּה, יְיָ אֱלֹהֵינוּ, מֶלֶךְ הָעוֹלָם,
אֲשֶׁר קִדְּשָׁנוּ בְּמִצְוֹתָיו וְצִוָּנוּ לַעֲסֹק בְּדִבְרֵי תוֹרָה.

הָעֲבוֹדָה "the worship"

הָעֲבוֹדָה is made up of two parts.

הָ means _____.

עֲבוֹדָה means "worship" or "service to God."

הָעֲבוֹדָה means _____.

The root of עֲבוֹדָה is עבד.

When a word has the root עבד, this tells us that "worship" or "work" is part of its meaning.

In each sentence below circle the word with the root עבד. Practice reading the sentences aloud.

1. מִי שֶׁעָשָׂה נִסִּים לַאֲבוֹתֵינוּ וְגָאַל אוֹתָם מֵעַבְדוּת לְחֵרוּת.

2. הַלְלוּיָהּ; הַלְלוּ, עַבְדֵי יְיָ, הַלְלוּ אֶת שֵׁם יְיָ.

3. עַל הַתּוֹרָה, וְעַל הָעֲבוֹדָה, וְעַל הַנְּבִיאִים, וְעַל יוֹם הַשַּׁבָּת הַזֶּה.

4. וּתְהִי לְרָצוֹן תָּמִיד עֲבוֹדַת יִשְׂרָאֵל עַמֶּךָ.

5. בָּרוּךְ אַתָּה יְיָ, הַבּוֹחֵר בַּתּוֹרָה, וּבְמֹשֶׁה עַבְדּוֹ.

There are two kinds of mitzvot in the Torah—mitzvot that people do to serve God (ritual mitzvot), and mitzvot that people do to serve one another (ethical mitzvot).

Here are two examples of mitzvot we do to serve God.
Can you think of two more?

1. Light Shabbat candles   3. _____

2. Eat a meal in a sukkah   4. _____

גְּמִילוּת חֲסָדִים "acts of loving-kindness"

חֲסָדִים is the plural of חֶסֶד.

חֶסֶד means "good deed" or "act of loving-kindness."

חֲסָדִים means "good deeds" or "acts of loving-kindness."

Circle the part of the word that shows it is plural.   חֲסָדִים

Here are two examples of mitzvot we do to serve other people.

Can you think of two more?

1. Give tzedakah   3. _____

2. Feed the hungry   4. _____

58

FLUENT READING

Each line below contains a word you know. Practice reading the lines.

1. תְּהִלַּת יְיָ יְדַבֶּר פִּי, וִיבָרֵךְ כָּל בָּשָׂר שֵׁם קָדְשׁוֹ לְעוֹלָם וָעֶד.

2. וּדְבַר אֶחָד מִדְּבָרֶיךָ אָחוֹר לֹא יָשׁוּב רֵיקָם.

3. בֵּינִי וּבֵין בְּנֵי יִשְׂרָאֵל אוֹת הִיא לְעֹלָם.

4. שֶׁלֹּא עָשָׂנוּ כְּגוֹיֵי הָאֲרָצוֹת וְלֹא שָׂמָנוּ כְּמִשְׁפְּחוֹת הָאֲדָמָה.

5. שְׁלֹשָׁה מִי יוֹדֵעַ? שְׁלֹשָׁה אֲנִי יוֹדֵעַ. שְׁלֹשָׁה אָבוֹת, שְׁנֵי לֻחוֹת הַבְּרִית, אֶחָד אֱלֹהֵינוּ שֶׁבַּשָּׁמַיִם וּבָאָרֶץ.

6. וּלְקַיֵּם אֶת כָּל דִּבְרֵי תַלְמוּד תּוֹרָתֶךָ בְּאַהֲבָה.

7. בָּרוּךְ אַתָּה, יְיָ, גּוֹמֵל חֲסָדִים טוֹבִים לְעַמּוֹ יִשְׂרָאֵל.

In what ways can someone pledge loyalty? Soldiers in the military promise to defend their country. A bride and groom pledge their loyalty to each other under the *ḥuppah*. You and your best friend might make a pact to stay best friends forever.

For the Jewish people, עָלֵינוּ, one of the concluding prayers of the service, is a pledge of loyalty to God. In it, we praise God as the one Creator and Ruler, and we unite in our recognition of our one God. During the prayer, we bend our knees and bow to show our respect and honor for God.

Practice reading these excerpts from עָלֵינוּ aloud.

1. עָלֵינוּ לְשַׁבֵּחַ לַאֲדוֹן הַכֹּל, לָתֵת גְּדֻלָּה לְיוֹצֵר בְּרֵאשִׁית...

2. וַאֲנַחְנוּ כּוֹרְעִים וּמִשְׁתַּחֲוִים וּמוֹדִים לִפְנֵי מֶלֶךְ מַלְכֵי הַמְּלָכִים, הַקָּדוֹשׁ בָּרוּךְ הוּא...

3. וְנֶאֱמַר: וְהָיָה יְיָ לְמֶלֶךְ עַל־כָּל־הָאָרֶץ בַּיּוֹם הַהוּא יִהְיֶה יְיָ אֶחָד וּשְׁמוֹ אֶחָד.

It is our duty to praise the God of all, to praise the Creator of the universe...
We bend the knee, bow, and give thanks before the Ruler of rulers,
the Holy One, who is blessed...
And it is said: Adonai will rule all the land.
On that day, Adonai will be One and God's name will be One.

PRAYER DICTIONARY

עָלֵינוּ
it is our duty

לְשַׁבֵּחַ
to praise

(לַ)אֲדוֹן
God

הַכֹּל
of all

וַאֲנַחְנוּ
and we

וּמוֹדִים
and thank

מֶלֶךְ מַלְכֵי הַמְּלָכִים
Ruler of rulers

הָאָרֶץ
the land

בַּיּוֹם הַהוּא
on that day

יִהְיֶה
will be

FREE CHOICE

Pick four words from the Prayer Dictionary and write them below in Hebrew and English.

English	Hebrew	
_____	_____	.1
_____	_____	.2
_____	_____	.3
_____	_____	.4

A bride and groom pledge their loyalty to one another under a *ḥuppah*.

PRAYER BACKGROUND

עָלֵינוּ is one of our most ancient prayers. We are not sure who wrote it or when, but we believe it is about 2,000 years old. In the third century C.E., עָלֵינוּ was included in the Rosh Hashanah service, and around the 13th century it became part of the daily prayer service. עָלֵינוּ came to be recited by Jewish men and women who, over the centuries, were condemned to death for refusing to convert to other religions. These Jews defiantly sang out their belief in one God and the greatness of God, and their hope for a perfect world.

VOCABULARY REVIEW

You have already learned many of the words in the עָלֵינוּ prayer.
Here is a list of some of the familiar words.

11. גְּדֻלָּה	6. לְ, לַ	1. עָלֵינוּ
12. הַכֹּל (כָּל)	7. וְעַל	2. מֶלֶךְ
13. מוֹדִים	8. לִפְנֵי	3. בְּרֵאשִׁית
14. אֶחָד	9. וּשְׁמוֹ (שֵׁם)	4. בָּרוּךְ
	10. הַקָּדוֹשׁ (קִדְּשָׁנוּ)	5. לָתֵת (נָתַן, נוֹתֵן)

In each prayer excerpt below, underline the words that appear in the
list above. Circle each word on the list as you find it in the prayer
excerpt. Then read each line.

1. בָּרוּךְ אַתָּה, יְיָ אֱלֹהֵינוּ, מֶלֶךְ הָעוֹלָם

2. הוּא יַעֲשֶׂה שָׁלוֹם עָלֵינוּ וְעַל כָּל יִשְׂרָאֵל

3. אֲשֶׁר שָׂם מֹשֶׁה לִפְנֵי בְּנֵי יִשְׂרָאֵל

4. זִכָּרוֹן לְמַעֲשֵׂה בְרֵאשִׁית

5. בָּרוּךְ אַתָּה יְיָ, נוֹתֵן הַתּוֹרָה

6. לְךָ יְיָ הַגְּדֻלָּה וְהַגְּבוּרָה

7. אֲשֶׁר קִדְּשָׁנוּ בְּמִצְוֹתָיו

8. יְיָ אֱלֹהֵינוּ, יְיָ אֶחָד

9. בָּרוּךְ שֵׁם כְּבוֹד מַלְכוּתוֹ

10. מוֹדִים אֲנַחְנוּ לָךְ

Prayer Building Blocks

עָלֵינוּ לְשַׁבֵּחַ לַאֲדוֹן הַכֹּל

"it is our duty to praise the God of all"

עָלֵינוּ לְשַׁבֵּחַ means "it is our duty to praise."

Who are we praising in עָלֵינוּ? _____

The word עָלֵינוּ, we have learned, means "on us" or "for us."

Read the following excerpt from the prayer עֹשֶׂה שָׁלוֹם.

הוּא יַעֲשֶׂה שָׁלוֹם עָלֵינוּ וְעַל כָּל יִשְׂרָאֵל

God will make peace for us and for all Israel.

But in the עָלֵינוּ prayer, in order to make the sentence flow, we translate the word עָלֵינוּ as: "It is our duty."

וַאֲנַחְנוּ כּוֹרְעִים וּמִשְׁתַּחֲוִים וּמוֹדִים

"and we bend the knee and bow and thank God"

כּוֹרְעִים וּמִשְׁתַּחֲוִים means "bend the knee and bow."

וּמוֹדִים means "and give thanks."

וּ means _____.

מוֹדִים means _____.

Do you know the word תּוֹדָה? What does it mean? _____

What is the connection to the word מוֹדִים? _____

HOW TO BOW

When we recite עָלֵינוּ, we bend our knees at the word כּוֹרְעִים, bow slightly at the word וּמִשְׁתַּחֲוִים, and then stand upright at the word לִפְנֵי. In this way we act out the words of the prayer.

Write the name of another prayer in which we bow to God.

(Hint: It's also called the Standing Prayer.) _____

Why do you think we bow during these prayers?

_____

לִפְנֵי מֶלֶךְ מַלְכֵי הַמְּלָכִים **"before the Ruler of rulers"**

לִפְנֵי means "before."

We bow down before the *Ruler of rulers.*

Write the three Hebrew words that mean "Ruler of rulers."

_____ _____ _____

Each of these words has the root ____ ____ ____.

Who is מֶלֶךְ מַלְכֵי הַמְּלָכִים? _____

This boy joins the community in support of Israel at an Israel Day Parade.

בַּיּוֹם הַהוּא יִהְיֶה יְיָ אֶחָד וּשְׁמוֹ אֶחָד

"on that day, Adonai will be one and God's name will be one"

בַּיּוֹם הַהוּא means "on that day."

יוֹם means "day."

Read the names of the days of the week in Hebrew.

Fill in the missing English word.

יוֹם חֲמִישִׁי	יוֹם רְבִיעִי	יוֹם שְׁלִישִׁי	יוֹם שֵׁנִי	יוֹם רִאשׁוֹן
Thursday	Wednesday	Tuesday	Monday	Sunday

יוֹם שִׁשִּׁי	יוֹם שַׁבָּת
Friday	_____

PRAYING TOGETHER

When we say עָלֵינוּ together we are praying as a community. Many words in עָלֵינוּ end with the suffix נוּ ("us" or "our"). Praying together as a group can give us a feeling of belonging to the congregation. We realize we are not alone in our prayers.

Below are the first lines of עָלֵינוּ. Circle all the words with the suffix נוּ.

1. עָלֵינוּ לְשַׁבֵּחַ לַאֲדוֹן הַכֹּל, לָתֵת גְּדֻלָּה לְיוֹצֵר בְּרֵאשִׁית,

2. שֶׁלֹּא עָשָׂנוּ כְּגוֹיֵי הָאֲרָצוֹת וְלֹא שָׂמָנוּ כְּמִשְׁפְּחוֹת

3. הָאֲדָמָה, שֶׁלֹּא שָׂם חֶלְקֵנוּ כָּהֶם וְגֹרָלֵנוּ כְּכָל־הֲמוֹנָם.

How many words did you circle? _____

Why do you think it is important to pray as a community?

_____

_____

_____

65

An Ethical Echo

The Book of Genesis tells us that God's greatest creations were man and woman, who were created in God's image—בְּצֶלֶם אֱלֹהִים. Our tradition teaches us that by *image*, we don't mean physical appearance—since God has no physical form—but rather, God's attributes of wisdom, kindness, righteousness, and fairness.

Think About This!

We are all created in God's image, but what does this mean? It means that we are all created with the ability to reflect God's ways, and to choose between right and wrong. Why, then, is it sometimes hard for us to treat everyone with the same respect and tolerance? If one of your classmates wears unusual clothing or needs a cane to get around school, you may feel uncomfortable. Perhaps you even treat this classmate differently as a result. What do you think the expression "beauty is only skin deep" means? Can you think of other expressions that have the same message? What are they?

Make up your own expression and explain it below.

_____

_____

_____

_____

It is important to be well groomed, but it is even more important to take the actions that make us beautiful inside.

FLUENT READING

Practice reading the following verses from עָלֵינוּ.

1. עָלֵינוּ לְשַׁבֵּחַ לַאֲדוֹן הַכֹּל, לָתֵת גְּדֻלָּה לְיוֹצֵר בְּרֵאשִׁית,

2. שֶׁלֹּא עָשָׂנוּ כְּגוֹיֵי הָאֲרָצוֹת וְלֹא שָׂמָנוּ כְּמִשְׁפְּחוֹת

3. הָאֲדָמָה, שֶׁלֹּא שָׂם חֶלְקֵנוּ כָּהֶם, וְגוֹרָלֵנוּ כְּכָל-הֲמוֹנָם.

4. וַאֲנַחְנוּ כּוֹרְעִים וּמִשְׁתַּחֲוִים וּמוֹדִים

5. לִפְנֵי מֶלֶךְ מַלְכֵי הַמְּלָכִים, הַקָּדוֹשׁ בָּרוּךְ הוּא,

6. שֶׁהוּא נוֹטֶה שָׁמַיִם וְיוֹסֵד אָרֶץ, וּמוֹשַׁב יְקָרוֹ בַּשָּׁמַיִם

7. מִמַּעַל, וּשְׁכִינַת עֻזּוֹ בְּגָבְהֵי מְרוֹמִים. הוּא אֱלֹהֵינוּ, אֵין

8. עוֹד. אֱמֶת מַלְכֵּנוּ, אֶפֶס זוּלָתוֹ, כַּכָּתוּב בְּתוֹרָתוֹ: וְיָדַעְתָּ

9. הַיּוֹם וַהֲשֵׁבֹתָ אֶל לְבָבֶךָ, כִּי יְיָ הוּא הָאֱלֹהִים בַּשָּׁמַיִם

10. מִמַּעַל וְעַל הָאָרֶץ מִתָּחַת, אֵין עוֹד.

11. וְנֶאֱמַר: וְהָיָה יְיָ לְמֶלֶךְ עַל כָּל-הָאָרֶץ, בַּיּוֹם הַהוּא

12. יִהְיֶה יְיָ אֶחָד וּשְׁמוֹ אֶחָד.

קַדִּישׁ

How unusual would a love song be if it didn't mention love? Or a movie about surfing that didn't show one surfboard? Surprisingly, the Mourner's קַדִּישׁ, a prayer said in memory of those who have died, doesn't mention death at all. Instead, it praises God, speaks of God's holiness, and expresses our longing for peace on earth. At our saddest moments, we speak words of promise and of hope.

Practice reading the Mourner's Kaddish aloud.

1. יִתְגַּדַּל וְיִתְקַדַּשׁ שְׁמֵהּ רַבָּא

2. בְּעָלְמָא דִּי בְרָא כִרְעוּתֵהּ, וְיַמְלִיךְ מַלְכוּתֵהּ

3. בְּחַיֵּיכוֹן וּבְיוֹמֵיכוֹן וּבְחַיֵּי דְכָל־בֵּית יִשְׂרָאֵל,

4. בַּעֲגָלָא וּבִזְמַן קָרִיב, וְאִמְרוּ אָמֵן.

5. יְהֵא שְׁמֵהּ רַבָּא מְבָרַךְ לְעָלַם וּלְעָלְמֵי עָלְמַיָּא.

6. יִתְבָּרַךְ וְיִשְׁתַּבַּח וְיִתְפָּאַר וְיִתְרוֹמַם וְיִתְנַשֵּׂא

7. וְיִתְהַדָּר וְיִתְעַלֶּה וְיִתְהַלָּל שְׁמֵהּ דְּקֻדְשָׁא, בְּרִיךְ הוּא.

8. לְעֵלָּא מִן כָּל־בִּרְכָתָא וְשִׁירָתָא,

9. תֻּשְׁבְּחָתָא וְנֶחֱמָתָא דַּאֲמִירָן בְּעָלְמָא, וְאִמְרוּ אָמֵן.

10. יְהֵא שְׁלָמָא רַבָּא מִן שְׁמַיָּא

11. וְחַיִּים עָלֵינוּ וְעַל־כָּל־יִשְׂרָאֵל, וְאִמְרוּ אָמֵן.

12. עֹשֶׂה שָׁלוֹם בִּמְרוֹמָיו הוּא יַעֲשֶׂה שָׁלוֹם

13. עָלֵינוּ וְעַל־כָּל־יִשְׂרָאֵל, וְאִמְרוּ אָמֵן.

Judaism teaches us the importance of comforting those who have suffered a loss, for them *and* for us.

May God's name be great and may it be made holy
in the world created according to God's will. May God rule
in our own lives and our own days, and in the life of all the house of Israel,
swiftly and soon, and say, Amen.
May God's great name be blessed forever and ever.
Blessed, praised, glorified, exalted, extolled,
honored, magnified, and adored be the name of the Holy One, blessed is God,
though God is beyond all the blessings, songs,
adorations, and consolations that are spoken in the world, and say, Amen.
May there be great peace from heaven
and life for us and for all Israel, and say, Amen.
May God who makes peace in the heavens, make peace
for us and for all Israel. And say, Amen.

DID YOU KNOW?

Did you notice something different about the language of the קַדִּישׁ? Most of the words in the קַדִּישׁ are Aramaic. Aramaic is a language similar to Hebrew that was spoken by the Jews at the time of Ezra in the fifth century B.C.E. and for about a thousand years thereafter. The last two lines of the קַדִּישׁ are written in Hebrew. Do you recognize them?

THE HEBREW-ARAMAIC CONNECTION

The words in the Kaddish may look difficult but, in fact, you already know many of them!

In the right-hand column are Hebrew prayer words you have already learned. In the left-hand column are related Aramaic words from the Kaddish.

Write the number of the Hebrew word next to its related Aramaic word. *(Hint: Look for related roots.)*

ARAMAIC		HEBREW	
בְּרִיךְ	_____	גְּדֻלָּה	1.
בְּעָלְמָא	_____	קִדְּשָׁנוּ	2.
וּבְחַיֵּי	_____	הָעוֹלָם	3.
יִתְגַּדַּל	_____	מֶלֶךְ	4.
קַדִּישׁ, וְיִתְקַדַּשׁ	_____	חַיִּים	5.
וְיַמְלִיךְ	_____	בָּרוּךְ	6.
שְׁלָמָא	_____	שָׁלוֹם	7.

קַדִּישׁ
holy

יִתְגַּדַּל
will be great

וְיִתְקַדַּשׁ
and will be holy

שְׁמֵהּ
God's name

בְּעָלְמָא
in the world

וְיַמְלִיךְ
and will rule

מַלְכוּתֵהּ
God's kingdom

וּבְחַיֵּי

and in the life of

לְעָלַם

forever

וְיִשְׁתַּבַּח

and will be praised

בְּרִיךְ

blessed

בְּרְכָתָא

blessing

שְׁלָמָא

peace

ROOT SEARCH

Write the root for each of the Aramaic words below.

ROOT	ARAMAIC WORD
___ ___ ___	בְּרִיךְ
___ ___ ___	מַלְכוּתֵהּ
___ ___ ___	יִתְגַּדַּל
___ ___ ___	בְּרְכָתָא
___ ___ ___	וְיַמְלִיךְ
___ ___ ___	קַדִּישׁ, וְיִתְקַדַּשׁ
___ ___ ___	שְׁלָמָא

Choose any four roots from above and write the English meaning.

ENGLISH MEANING	ROOT
_____	___ ___ ___
_____	___ ___ ___
_____	___ ___ ___
_____	___ ___ ___

WORD MATCH

Draw a line from the Aramaic word to its English meaning.

forever	קַדִּישׁ
(God's) kingdom	בְּרִיךְ
holy	לְעָלַם
blessed	מַלְכוּתֵהּ

(God's) name	שְׁלָמָא
and will be praised	שְׁמֵהּ
will be great	וְיִשְׁתַּבַּח
peace	יִתְגַּדַּל

and will be holy	בִּרְכָתָא
and will rule	וּבְחַיֵּי
blessing	וְיַמְלִיךְ
and in the life of	וְיִתְקַדַּשׁ

How, in a time of mourning, might paying attention to the grandeur of nature fill us with hope?

THE THEME OF THE PRAYER

We have learned that the Mourner's Kaddish is said in memory of someone who has died, yet it contains no mention of death.

Reread the English translation of the Kaddish on page 69. Pay attention to the tone and mood of the prayer. Then do the following exercise.

1. Fill in the blank by choosing the correct word.

   The Kaddish is a prayer of _____ to God. (thanks/praise/request)

2. Choose four words from the English translation of the prayer that illustrate your answer to number 1.

   _____ _____ _____ _____

3. The Kaddish ends on a hopeful, optimistic note.
   It ends with a wish for _____.
   Why do you think the Kaddish ends with this wish?

   _____

4. Why do you think the Kaddish is recited by mourners even though it does not mention death?

   _____

   _____

   _____

KADDISH QUIZ

Read the קַדִּישׁ and find the answers to the questions that appear on the opposite page.

1. יִתְגַּדַּל וְיִתְקַדַּשׁ שְׁמֵהּ רַבָּא

2. בְּעָלְמָא דִּי בְרָא כִרְעוּתֵהּ, וְיַמְלִיךְ מַלְכוּתֵהּ

3. בְּחַיֵּיכוֹן וּבְיוֹמֵיכוֹן וּבְחַיֵּי דְכָל־בֵּית יִשְׂרָאֵל,

4. בַּעֲגָלָא וּבִזְמַן קָרִיב, וְאִמְרוּ אָמֵן.

5. יְהֵא שְׁמֵהּ רַבָּא מְבָרַךְ לְעָלַם וּלְעָלְמֵי עָלְמַיָּא.

6. יִתְבָּרַךְ וְיִשְׁתַּבַּח וְיִתְפָּאַר וְיִתְרוֹמַם וְיִתְנַשֵּׂא

7. וְיִתְהַדָּר וְיִתְעַלֶּה וְיִתְהַלָּל שְׁמֵהּ דְּקֻדְשָׁא, בְּרִיךְ הוּא.

8. לְעֵלָּא מִן כָּל־בִּרְכָתָא וְשִׁירָתָא,

9. תֻּשְׁבְּחָתָא וְנֶחֱמָתָא דַּאֲמִירָן בְּעָלְמָא, וְאִמְרוּ אָמֵן.

10. יְהֵא שְׁלָמָא רַבָּא מִן שְׁמַיָּא

11. וְחַיִּים עָלֵינוּ וְעַל־כָּל־יִשְׂרָאֵל, וְאִמְרוּ אָמֵן.

12. עֹשֶׂה שָׁלוֹם בִּמְרוֹמָיו הוּא יַעֲשֶׂה שָׁלוֹם

13. עָלֵינוּ וְעַל־כָּל־יִשְׂרָאֵל, וְאִמְרוּ אָמֵן.

1. (Circle) all the words in the קַדִּישׁ that have the root קדשׁ.

   How many words did you circle? _____

   What does the root קדשׁ mean? _____

2. Put a ★ star above all the words with the root ברכ.

   How many words did you star? _____

   What does the root ברכ mean? _____

3. Three words in the קַדִּישׁ mean "life." Write them here.

   _____   _____   _____

4. Peace is an important concept in the קַדִּישׁ. Write the Hebrew word

   for "peace." _____

   This word—or a variation—appears three times near the end of the קַדִּישׁ.

   Put a box around each one.

5. We know that כָּל means _____.

   Now underline כָּל or כָּל wherever it appears.

   How many underlined words do you have? _____

6. עוֹלָם means "forever" or "world." This word appears five times, in a

   variety of forms, in the קַדִּישׁ.

   Write the five words here.

   _____   _____   _____

   _____   _____

ABOUT THE KADDISH

In this chapter we have learned about the Mourner's קַדִּישׁ. But there are other versions of the קַדִּישׁ, for example the חֲצִי קַדִּישׁ ("half Kaddish"), which is only slightly shorter. The קַדִּישׁ divides up the service, almost the way a file divider separates the subjects in your school binder. It indicates the end of one section of the service and the beginning of the next.

We are not sure who wrote the קַדִּישׁ or when. It probably developed over hundreds of years. We do know that almost 800 years ago the קַדִּישׁ came to be the prayer said by mourners.

In some congregations, only the mourners and those observing *yahrzeit*—the anniversary of a loved one's death—stand as they recite the קַדִּישׁ. In other congregations, everyone stands as a sign of support for the mourners and to remember those who died in the Holocaust.

We say the קַדִּישׁ only in the presence of a מִנְיָן. As the mourners rhythmically chant the prayer, the congregation publicly acknowledges God's greatness. Although the Mourner's קַדִּישׁ is recited in memory of the dead, its words also give strength to the living.

Below are the last two lines of the קַדִּישׁ.

עֹשֶׂה שָׁלוֹם בִּמְרוֹמָיו הוּא יַעֲשֶׂה שָׁלוֹם
עָלֵינוּ וְעַל־כָּל־יִשְׂרָאֵל, וְאִמְרוּ אָמֵן.

May God who makes peace in the heavens, make peace for us and for all Israel. And say, Amen.

עֹשֶׂה שָׁלוֹם is the same sentence that concludes both the עֲמִידָה and בִּרְכַּת הַמָּזוֹן (Grace After Meals). When we say עֹשֶׂה שָׁלוֹם at the end of the קַדִּישׁ and the עֲמִידָה, it is traditional to take three steps backward, then to bow to the left, to the right, and then forward. It is as if the person praying is leaving the presence of a king or a queen. Who is the Ruler whose presence we are leaving? _____

Answer the following questions in Hebrew:

1. In עֹשֶׂה שָׁלוֹם, what do we ask God for? _____

2. For whom do we want peace? _____

FLUENT READING

Each line below contains a word or phrase you know. Practice reading the lines.

1. תִּתְגַּדַּל וְתִתְקַדַּשׁ בְּתוֹךְ יְרוּשָׁלַיִם עִירֶךָ.

2. לְדוֹר וָדוֹר נַגִּיד גָּדְלֶךָ, וּלְנֵצַח נְצָחִים קְדֻשָּׁתְךָ נַקְדִּישׁ.

3. גָּדוֹל יְיָ וּמְהֻלָּל מְאֹד וְלִגְדֻלָּתוֹ אֵין חֵקֶר.

4. וְשִׁבְחֲךָ אֱלֹהֵינוּ מִפִּינוּ לֹא יָמוּשׁ לְעוֹלָם וָעֶד.

5. עָלֵינוּ לְשַׁבֵּחַ לַאֲדוֹן הַכֹּל לָתֵת גְּדֻלָּה לְיוֹצֵר בְּרֵאשִׁית.

6. יִגְדַּל אֱלֹהִים חַי וְיִשְׁתַּבַּח.

7. מַלְכוּתְךָ מַלְכוּת כָּל עֹלָמִים, וּמֶמְשַׁלְתְּךָ בְּכָל דּוֹר וָדֹר.

8. הַבָּא עָלֵינוּ וְעַל כָּל יִשְׂרָאֵל לְטוֹבָה.

9. כִּי הַמַּלְכוּת שֶׁלְּךָ הִיא וּלְעוֹלְמֵי עַד תִּמְלוֹךְ בְּכָבוֹד.

10. בָּרְכוּנִי לְשָׁלוֹם מַלְאֲכֵי הַשָּׁלוֹם מַלְאֲכֵי עֶלְיוֹן.

אֵין כֵּאלֹהֵינוּ

Think about your favorite music. Why do you want to hear it over and over again? It could be the lyrics, the voice of the singer, the driving beat, or a memory it brings back. The אֵין כֵּאלֹהֵינוּ hymn, sung at the conclusion of the service, has a joyful, repetitive rhythm that unites the voices of the congregation. Listen carefully the next time you hear it sung—it's hard not to join in! As we raise our voices to sing אֵין כֵּאלֹהֵינוּ, we honor God in four ways—as our God, our Sovereign, our Ruler, and our Savior.

Practice reading אֵין כֵּאלֹהֵינוּ aloud.

1. אֵין כֵּאלֹהֵינוּ,	אֵין כַּאדוֹנֵינוּ,
2. אֵין כְּמַלְכֵּנוּ,	אֵין כְּמוֹשִׁיעֵנוּ.
3. מִי כֵאלֹהֵינוּ,	מִי כַאדוֹנֵינוּ,
4. מִי כְמַלְכֵּנוּ,	מִי כְמוֹשִׁיעֵנוּ.
5. נוֹדֶה לֵאלֹהֵינוּ,	נוֹדֶה לַאדוֹנֵינוּ,
6. נוֹדֶה לְמַלְכֵּנוּ,	נוֹדֶה לְמוֹשִׁיעֵנוּ.
7. בָּרוּךְ אֱלֹהֵינוּ,	בָּרוּךְ אֲדוֹנֵינוּ,
8. בָּרוּךְ מַלְכֵּנוּ,	בָּרוּךְ מוֹשִׁיעֵנוּ.
9. אַתָּה הוּא אֱלֹהֵינוּ,	אַתָּה הוּא אֲדוֹנֵינוּ,
10. אַתָּה הוּא מַלְכֵּנוּ,	אַתָּה הוּא מוֹשִׁיעֵנוּ.

There is none like our God,
There is none like our Ruler,
Who is like our God?
Who is like our Ruler?
We will give thanks to our God,
We will give thanks to our Ruler,
Blessed is our God,
Blessed is our Ruler,
You are our God,
You are our Ruler,

There is none like our Sovereign,
There is none like our Savior.
Who is like our Sovereign?
Who is like our Savior?
We will give thanks to our Sovereign,
We will give thanks to our Savior.
Blessed is our Sovereign,
Blessed is our Savior.
You are our Sovereign,
You are our Savior.

אֵין כְּ

there is none like

מִי כְ

who is like

נוֹדֶה לְ

we will give thanks to

אַתָּה הוּא

you are

אֱלֹהֵינוּ

our God

אֲדוֹנֵינוּ

our sovereign

מַלְכֵּנוּ

our ruler

מוֹשִׁיעֵנוּ

our savior

SEARCH AND CIRCLE

Circle the Hebrew word that means the same as the English.

our savior	אָבִינוּ	אֱלֹהֵינוּ	מוֹשִׁיעֵנוּ
there is none like	בָּרוּךְ שֶׁ	אֵין כְּ	אַתָּה הוּא
our sovereign	אֲדוֹנֵינוּ	אֱלֹהֵינוּ	אֲבוֹתֵינוּ
our ruler	מַלְכֵּנוּ	קִדְּשָׁנוּ	אֱלֹהֵינוּ
we will give thanks to	בָּרְכוּ אֶת	נוֹדֶה לְ	לְעַמּוֹ
you are	יְיָ אֶחָד אַתָּה הוּא	עָלֵינוּ
our God	מַלְכוּתוֹ	וְצִוָּנוּ	אֱלֹהֵינוּ
who is like	כִּי בָנוּ	נוֹדֶה לְ	מִי כְ

Joyous music can magically bring voices—and clapping hands—together.

ARCHITECTURE OF THE PRAYER

See how carefully structured אֵין כֵּאלֹהֵינוּ is.

Read the prayer across, line by line, then complete the activities that follow.

אֵין כַּאדוֹנֵינוּ,	1. אֵין כֵּאלֹהֵינוּ,
אֵין כְּמוֹשִׁיעֵנוּ.	2. אֵין כְּמַלְכֵּנוּ,
מִי כַאדוֹנֵינוּ,	3. מִי כֵאלֹהֵינוּ,
מִי כְמוֹשִׁיעֵנוּ.	4. מִי כְמַלְכֵּנוּ,
נוֹדֶה לַאדוֹנֵינוּ,	5. נוֹדֶה לֵאלֹהֵינוּ,
נוֹדֶה לְמוֹשִׁיעֵנוּ.	6. נוֹדֶה לְמַלְכֵּנוּ,
בָּרוּךְ אֲדוֹנֵינוּ,	7. בָּרוּךְ אֱלֹהֵינוּ,
בָּרוּךְ מוֹשִׁיעֵנוּ.	8. בָּרוּךְ מַלְכֵּנוּ,
אַתָּה הוּא אֲדוֹנֵינוּ,	9. אַתָּה הוּא אֱלֹהֵינוּ,
אַתָּה הוּא מוֹשִׁיעֵנוּ.	10. אַתָּה הוּא מַלְכֵּנוּ,

1. Circle אֵין each time it appears.

2. Underline מִי each time it appears.

3. Put a box around נוֹדֶה each time it appears.

In the spaces below, write the initial letters of the following words from אֵין כֵּאלֹהֵינוּ to spell out a new, "secret" word:

אֵין   מִי   נוֹדֶה

(Remember: נ at the end of a word is written ן.)

_____ _____ _____

Did you figure out the secret word? When do we say this word?

Prayer Building Blocks

אֵין כְּ "there is none like"

אֵין means "there is none."

כְּ is a prefix that means "like."

אֵין כְּ means _____.

Circle the Hebrew word and prefix meaning "there is none like" in the lines below.

אֵין כֵּאלֹהֵינוּ   אֵין כַּאדוֹנֵינוּ

אֵין כְּמַלְכֵּנוּ   אֵין כְּמוֹשִׁיעֵנוּ

מִי כְּ "who is like"

מִי means "who is."

כְּ means "like."

Circle the word and prefix meaning "who is like" in the lines below.

מִי כֵּאלֹהֵינוּ   מִי כַאדוֹנֵינוּ

מִי כְמַלְכֵּנוּ   מִי כְמוֹשִׁיעֵנוּ

נוֹדֶה לְ "we will give thanks to"

נוֹדֶה means "we will give thanks."

לְ is a prefix that means _____.

Circle the word and prefix meaning "we will give thanks to" in the lines below.

נוֹדֶה לֵאלֹהֵינוּ   נוֹדֶה לַאדוֹנֵינוּ

נוֹדֶה לְמַלְכֵּנוּ   נוֹדֶה לְמוֹשִׁיעֵנוּ

אַתָּה הוּא "you are"

Circle the Hebrew words that mean "you are" in the lines below.

אַתָּה הוּא אֱלֹהֵינוּ   אַתָּה הוּא אֲדוֹנֵינוּ

אַתָּה הוּא מַלְכֵּנוּ   אַתָּה הוּא מוֹשִׁיעֵנוּ.

PREFIX REVIEW

In אֵין כֵּאלֹהֵינוּ, two prefixes are repeated. They are כ and ל. Circle the prefix in each of these words:

כֵּאלֹהֵינוּ   לַאדוֹנֵינוּ   לְמַלְכֵּנוּ   כְּמוֹשִׁיעֵנוּ

Write the meaning of each prefix.

כ _____

ל _____

SUFFIX REVIEW

אֱלֹהֵינוּ means "our God."

אֲדוֹנֵינוּ means "our sovereign."

מַלְכֵּנוּ means "our ruler."

מוֹשִׁיעֵנוּ means "our savior."

All of these words describing God end with the suffix _____.

Underline the suffix in each of the words above.

What does this suffix mean? _____.

Sometimes people look for easy solutions—an easy way out—but Judaism teaches us to strive for worthwhile goals and to work hard to reach them.

82

PUTTING IT TOGETHER

You know the beginning (prefix) and the ending (suffix) of each word below.

כְּמוֹשִׁיעֵנוּ   לְמַלְכֵּנוּ   לַאדוֹנֵינוּ   כֵּאלֹהֵינוּ

Write the number of the matching English meaning above each Hebrew word.

1. to our ruler
2. to our sovereign
3. like our savior
4. like our God

Now circle the main part (not the prefix or suffix) of each Hebrew word above. (The first one has been done for you.)

Each of these main parts is actually a name for God. You may not recognize them at first, because when a word has a prefix or suffix added, it may change its vowels or lose a final letter.

Connect the names for God in column 1 to the related words from אֵין כֵּאלֹהֵינוּ in column 2.

2	1	
אֱלֹהֵינוּ	מֶלֶךְ	_____
מַלְכֵּנוּ	אָדוֹן	_____
אֲדוֹנֵינוּ	מוֹשִׁיעַ	_____
מוֹשִׁיעֵנוּ	אֱלֹהִים	_____

Now write the English meaning for the words in column 1 in the blank spaces.

A HYMN OF PRAISE

אֵין כֵּאלֹהֵינוּ was written before the ninth century C.E. It is over 1,000 years old! אֵין כֵּאלֹהֵינוּ is an important statement of our belief in God.

Reread the English translation of אֵין כֵּאלֹהֵינוּ on page 78.

In your own words, describe the Jewish belief in God that is expressed in אֵין כֵּאלֹהֵינוּ.

_____

_____

_____

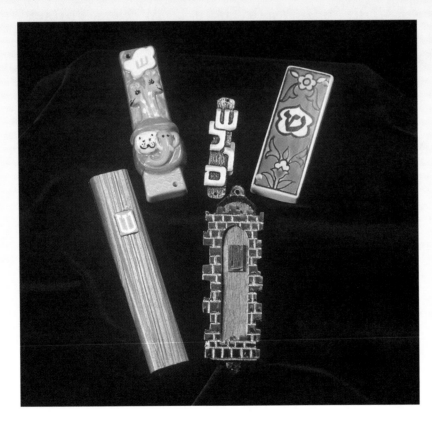

Although mezuzot may look different on the outside, inside, each mezuzah contains the same important statement of belief in God—the Sh'ma.

FLUENT READING

Each line below contains a word you know. Practice reading the lines.

1. מִי כַיָי אֱלֹהֵינוּ, הַמַּגְבִּיהִי לָשֶׁבֶת.

2. אָבִינוּ מַלְכֵּנוּ, שְׁמַע קוֹלֵנוּ.

3. אֵין גְּדֻלָּה כַּתּוֹרָה וְאֵין דּוֹרְשֶׁיהָ כְּיִשְׂרָאֵל.

4. הוּא מַלְכֵּנוּ. הוּא מוֹשִׁיעֵנוּ.

5. בָּרְכֵנוּ אָבִינוּ כֻּלָּנוּ כְּאֶחָד בְּאוֹר פָּנֶיךָ.

6. אֵין אַדִּיר כַּיָי, וְאֵין בָּרוּךְ כְּבֶן עַמְרָם.

7. אֶחָד הוּא אֱלֹהֵינוּ. הוּא אָבִינוּ.

8. בָּרוּךְ אַתָּה, יְיָ אֱלֹהֵינוּ, מֶלֶךְ הָעוֹלָם, הָאֵל, אָבִינוּ, מַלְכֵּנוּ.

9. אָבִינוּ מַלְכֵּנוּ, חַדֵּשׁ עָלֵינוּ שָׁנָה טוֹבָה.

10. שְׁמַע יִשְׂרָאֵל: יְיָ אֱלֹהֵינוּ, יְיָ אֶחָד.

הַשְׁכִּיבֵנוּ
שְׁמַע
מוֹדֶה אֲנִי

הַשְׁכִּיבֵנוּ

Have you ever noticed that tomorrow's big math test seems scarier when you wake up in the middle of the night and think about it? Or that the argument you had with your buddy can seem worse at 3 A.M. than in the light of day? As we get older, our daily problems and stresses may wake us up during the night and cause us to worry, often making the nighttime difficult.

In ancient times, people believed that our souls left our bodies during sleep and were restored to us by God upon our waking. The nighttime seemed frightening, and הַשְׁכִּיבֵנוּ, the second blessing after the evening Sh'ma, was written as a prayer for protection from harm overnight. This prayer asks God to shelter us with peace and to bring us safely through the night to a brand-new day.

1. הַשְׁכִּיבֵנוּ יְיָ אֱלֹהֵינוּ לְשָׁלוֹם, וְהַעֲמִידֵנוּ מַלְכֵּנוּ לְחַיִּים,

2. וּפְרוֹשׂ עָלֵינוּ סֻכַּת שְׁלוֹמֶךָ...

3. וּשְׁמוֹר צֵאתֵנוּ וּבוֹאֵנוּ

4. לְחַיִּים וּלְשָׁלוֹם מֵעַתָּה וְעַד עוֹלָם.

Make us lie down, Adonai, in peace, and stand us up again, our Ruler, to life,
and spread upon us the shelter of Your peace….
And guard our going and our coming,
for life and for peace now and forever.

הַשְׁכִּיבֵנוּ

make us lie down

וְהַעֲמִידֵנוּ

and make us stand up

סֻכַּת

the shelter of

שְׁלוֹמֶךָ

your peace

OPPOSITES ATTRACT

וְהַעֲמִידֵנוּ and הַשְׁכִּיבֵנוּ are opposites.

הַשְׁכִּיבֵנוּ means _____.

וְהַעֲמִידֵנוּ means _____.

The root of וְהַעֲמִידֵנוּ is עמד.

עמד tells us that "stand" is part of a word's meaning.

Circle the root letters in this word: עֲמִידָה

Do you recognize the word? It is the name of the prayer at the heart of most synagogue services.

Choose the correct word to complete the sentence.

We _____when we say the עֲמִידָה. (sit/stand)

At the end of a busy day, dusk can bring a quietness to the world. How do you feel as you watch the sun set?

TAKE SHELTER

הַשְׁכִּיבֵנוּ asks God to spread upon us "the shelter of Your peace"— סֻכַּת שְׁלוֹמֶךָ. You know both these Hebrew words. Connect each word from הַשְׁכִּיבֵנוּ on the right to its related word on the left.

שָׁלוֹם   סֻכַּת

סֻכָּה   שְׁלוֹמֶךָ

Why is "the shelter of Your peace" a good metaphor to use?

_____

_____

COMINGS AND GOINGS

הַשְׁכִּיבֵנוּ asks God to "guard our going and our coming"—
צֵאתֵנוּ וּבוֹאֵנוּ. (In English we use the expression the other way
around!) Below are two lines from שָׁלוֹם עֲלֵיכֶם that we sing at
home on Friday night between lighting the candles and reciting the
Kiddush. The lines contain words similar to צֵאתֵנוּ and וּבוֹאֵנוּ.

For each line from שָׁלוֹם עֲלֵיכֶם, circle the word that is related to
וּבוֹאֵנוּ or צֵאתֵנוּ.

בּוֹאֲכֶם לְשָׁלוֹם, מַלְאֲכֵי הַשָּׁלוֹם, מַלְאֲכֵי עֶלְיוֹן.

צֵאתְכֶם לְשָׁלוֹם, מַלְאֲכֵי הַשָּׁלוֹם, מַלְאֲכֵי עֶלְיוֹן.

THEME OF THE PRAYER

Look back at the English translation of הַשְׁכִּיבֵנוּ on page 86. In
your own words explain what we are praying for. Use words or
phrases from the prayer as examples.

_____

_____

_____

שְׁמַע

The שְׁמַע is the Jewish people's simple, complete, and ultimate declaration of faith in our one God. It is our pledge of loyalty to God. In it we express our belief in the one God, the God who created the entire universe.

The Sh'ma is such an important statement that we often recite it with our eyes closed to avoid distraction. We say the Sh'ma at night before going to sleep to end our day with an expression of loyalty to God. We say the Sh'ma in the morning to renew our commitment to God.

Practice reading the שְׁמַע aloud.

שְׁמַע יִשְׂרָאֵל: יְיָ אֱלֹהֵינוּ, יְיָ אֶחָד.

Hear O Israel: Adonai is our God, Adonai is One.

Why do you think we say the שְׁמַע in the synagogue *and* at home?

_____

_____

_____

מוֹדֶה אֲנִי

What do you look forward to when you start a new day? Waking up to get ready for school when the clock radio goes off may not always be fun. But our days are filled with the promise of good things for which we can be thankful—things like playing sports, getting a hug from our mom or dad, doing a favor for a friend, or catching the latest movie.

The מוֹדֶה אֲנִי prayer, said first thing upon awakening in the morning (even before getting out of bed), thanks God for returning our souls to us and for giving us a new day to live a rich, full life.

Practice reading the prayer aloud.

Boys and men say:

1. מוֹדֶה אֲנִי לְפָנֶיךָ מֶלֶךְ חַי וְקַיָּם שֶׁהֶחֱזַרְתָּ בִּי נִשְׁמָתִי
2. בְּחֶמְלָה רַבָּה אֱמוּנָתֶךָ.

Girls and women say:

1. מוֹדָה אֲנִי לְפָנֶיךָ מֶלֶךְ חַי וְקַיָּם שֶׁהֶחֱזַרְתָּ בִּי נִשְׁמָתִי
2. בְּחֶמְלָה רַבָּה אֱמוּנָתֶךָ.

I give thanks to You, living and everlasting Ruler, who has graciously returned my soul to me. Great is Your faithfulness!

מוֹדֶה\מוֹדָה

give thanks

אֲנִי

I

לְפָנֶיךָ

to you (before you)

מֶלֶךְ

(is) ruler

חַי

living

וְקַיָּם

and everlasting

MATCH THE MEANING

Connect each Hebrew word to its English meaning.

everlasting	מוֹדֶה\מוֹדָה
to you (before you)	אֲנִי
living	לְפָנֶיךָ
give thanks	מֶלֶךְ
ruler	חַי
I	וְקַיָּם

Whether we wake up with a big smile or are nervous about the day ahead, our tradition teaches us to appreciate the potential in each new day.

WHAT'S MISSING?

Fill in the missing words to complete each prayer phrase.

ו. מוֹדֶה\מוֹדָה _____ לְפָנֶיךָ

_____ give thanks to you

2. מֶלֶךְ _____ וְקַיָּם

_____ and everlasting ruler

FROM THE SOURCES

The second part of מוֹדֶה\מוֹדָה אֲנִי tells us that God's faithfulness is great (רַבָּה אֱמוּנָתֶךָ). The message of the abundance of God's faithfulness is taken from the Book of Lamentations (3:22-23). The Jewish people were in great pain over the destruction of the First Temple in 586 B.C.E. but were comforted by the belief that the grace of God continues nonetheless.

Read these lines from Lamentations and circle the two words that together mean "great is your faithfulness."

22 חַסְדֵי יְהוָֹה כִּי לֹא־תָֹמְנוּ
כִּי לֹא־כָלוּ רַחֲמָיו:
23 חֲדָשִׁים לַבְּקָרִים רַבָּה אֱמוּנָתֶךָ:

WRITE YOUR OWN PRAYER

מוֹדֶה\מוֹדָה אֲנִי expresses deep hope and optimism. It tells us: God's mercy and compassion are renewed for us each morning. Today is a new day. We are alive. We have another chance.

On the lines below, write your own prayer for the new day.

_____

_____

_____

_____

FLUENT READING

Each line below contains a word you know. Practice reading the lines.

1. וַאֲנַחְנוּ כּוֹרְעִים וּמִשְׁתַּחֲוִים וּמוֹדִים לִפְנֵי מֶלֶךְ מַלְכֵי הַמְּלָכִים, הַקָּדוֹשׁ בָּרוּךְ הוּא.

2. שָׁמוֹר וְזָכוֹר בְּדִבּוּר אֶחָד הִשְׁמִיעָנוּ אֵל הַמְיֻחָד

3. בַּיּוֹם הַהוּא יִהְיֶה יְיָ אֶחָד וּשְׁמוֹ אֶחָד.

4. בָּרוּךְ אַתָּה, יְיָ אֱלֹהֵינוּ, מֶלֶךְ הָעוֹלָם, אֲשֶׁר קִדְּשָׁנוּ בְּמִצְוֹתָיו וְצִוָּנוּ לֵישֵׁב בַּסֻּכָּה.

5. הַפּוֹרֵשׂ סֻכַּת שָׁלוֹם עָלֵינוּ, וְעַל כָּל עַמּוֹ יִשְׂרָאֵל, וְעַל יְרוּשָׁלָיִם.

6. שְׁמַע! בַּיָּמִים הָהֵם בַּזְּמַן הַזֶּה.

7. שָׁלוֹם עֲלֵיכֶם, מַלְאֲכֵי הַשָּׁרֵת, מַלְאֲכֵי עֶלְיוֹן.

8. נוֹדֶה לְךָ וּנְסַפֵּר תְּהִלָּתֶךָ.

9. שָׁלוֹם רָב עַל יִשְׂרָאֵל עַמְּךָ תָּשִׂים לְעוֹלָם.

10. מוֹדִים אֲנַחְנוּ לָךְ, שָׁאַתָּה הוּא יְיָ אֱלֹהֵינוּ.

Shabbat Morning Service

PRELIMINARY PRAYERS

מוֹדֶה אֲנִי

THE SH'MA AND ITS BLESSINGS

בָּרְכוּ

יוֹצֵר אוֹר

אַהֲבָה רַבָּה

שְׁמַע

וְאָהַבְתָּ

מִי כָמֹכָה

THE SHABBAT AMIDAH

אָבוֹת

אָבוֹת וְאִמָּהוֹת

גְּבוּרוֹת

קְדוּשָׁה

קְדוּשַׁת הַיּוֹם

עֲבוֹדָה

הוֹדָאָה

שִׂים שָׁלוֹם

עֹשֶׂה שָׁלוֹם

THE TORAH SERVICE

אֵין כָּמוֹךְ

אַב הָרַחֲמִים

כִּי מִצִּיוֹן

לְךָ יְיָ

בִּרְכוֹת הַתּוֹרָה

וְזֹאת הַתּוֹרָה

בִּרְכוֹת הַהַפְטָרָה

עֵץ חַיִּים הִיא

ADDITIONAL PRAYERS

עָלֵינוּ

קַדִּישׁ

אֵין כֵּאלֹהֵינוּ

א	אֲדוֹנֵינוּ	our sovereign
	אֵין	(there is) none
	אֵין כּ	there is none like
	אֱלֹהֵינוּ	our God
	אֱמֶת	truth
	אֲנִי	I
	אַתָּה הוּא	you are
ב	בֶּאֱמֶת	in truth
	בָּחַר	chose
	בָּטָחְנוּ	we trust(ed)
	בַּיּוֹם הַהוּא	on that day
	(בִּ)נְבִיאִים	prophets
	בָּנוּ	us
	בְּנֵי	people of
	בְּעָלְמָא	in the world
	בִּקְדֻשָּׁתוֹ	in God's holiness
	בְּרִיךְ	blessed
	בִּרְכָתָא	blessing
ג	גְּמִילוּת חֲסָדִים	acts of loving-kindness
ד	דְּבָרִים	things
	דַּרְכֵי	ways of
	דְּרָכֶיהָ	its ways
ה	הָאָרֶץ	the land
	הַבּוֹחֵר	the one who chooses
	הַכֹּל	of all
	הַנֶּאֱמָרִים	spoken
	הָעֲבוֹדָה	the worship
	הָעוֹלָם	the world
	הָעַמִּים	the nations
	הָרַחֲמִים	merciful, the mercy
	הַשְׁכִּיבֵנוּ	make us lie down
	הַתּוֹרָה	the Torah
ו	וַאֲנַחְנוּ	and we
	וּבְחַיֵּי	and in the life of
	וּדְבַר	and the word of
	וְהַעֲמִידֵנוּ	and make us stand up
	וְזֹאת	and this is
	וְחַיֵּי	and life (of)
	וְיַמְלִיךְ	and will rule
	וְיִשְׁתַּבַּח	and will be praised
	וְיִתְקַדַּשׁ	and will be holy
	וּמוֹדִים	and thank
	וּמֶמְשַׁלְתְּךָ	and your reign
	וְנָתַן	and gave (and giving)
	וָצֶדֶק	and righteousness (justice)
	וְקַיָּם	and everlasting
ח	חַי	living
	חַיִּים	(of) life
ט	טוֹבִים	good (faithful)
י	יִהְיֶה	will be
	יִמְלֹךְ	will rule
	יְרוּשָׁלַיִם	Jerusalem
	יִשְׂרָאֵל	Israel
	יִתְגַּדַּל	will be great
כ	כָּמוֹךָ	like you
	(כְּ)מַעֲשֶׂיךָ	(like) your deeds
ל	(לַ)אֲדוֹן	God
	לָנוּ	to us
	לְעָלַם	forever
	לְעַמּוֹ	to God's people
	לִפְנֵי	before
	לְפָנֶיךָ	to you (before you)
	לְשַׁבֵּחַ	to praise
מ	מְאֻשָּׁר	happy
	מוֹדֶה\מוֹדָה	give thanks
	מוֹשִׁיעֵנוּ	our savior
	מִי כ	who is like
	מִירוּשָׁלָיִם	from Jerusalem
	מִכָּל	from all
	מָלָךְ	ruled
	מֶלֶךְ	(is) ruler
	מֶלֶךְ מַלְכֵי הַמְּלָכִים	Ruler of rulers
	מַלְכוּתֵהּ	God's kingdom
	מַלְכוּתְךָ	your sovereignty
	מַלְכֵּנוּ	our ruler
	מִצִּיּוֹן	from Zion
	מֹשֶׁה	Moses
נ	נוֹדֶה ל	we will give thanks to
	נוֹתֵן	gives
	נֹעַם	pleasantness
ס	סֻכַּת	the shelter of
ע	עַבְדּוֹ	God's servant
	עוֹלָם	eternal, world
	עוֹמֵד	stands
	עַל	on
	עָלֵינוּ	it is our duty
	עַמּוֹ	God's people
	עֵץ	tree
ק	קַדִּישׁ	holy
ש	שָׁלוֹם	peace
	שְׁלוֹמֶךָ	your peace
	שְׁלָמָא	peace
	שְׁלשָׁה	three
	שָׂם	placed, put
	שְׁמֵהּ	God's name
	שֶׁנָּתַן	who gave
ת	תּוֹרָה	Torah, teaching
	תּוֹרַת	Torah of
	תּוֹרָתוֹ	God's Torah